D1709691

BUYING RURAL LAND IN TEXAS

*Publication of this book
is sponsored by a generous gift
in honor of Nancy Painter Paup,
beloved wife and constant partner
in all our many activities.*

Thaddeus (Ted) Paup '74

The publisher also acknowledges the support
of the Real Estate Center at Texas A&M University.

Buying Rural

CHARLES E. GILLILAND

and in Texas

TEXAS A&M UNIVERSITY PRESS   College Station

Manufactured in China by Everbest Printing Co.,
through FCI Print Group
Second Printing, 2017
This paper meets the requirements of ANSI/NISO Z39.48-1992
(Permanence of Paper).
Binding materials have been chosen for durability.
♾ ♻

Library of Congress Cataloging-in-Publication Data
Gilliland, Charles E. (Charles Edward)
Buying rural land in Texas / Charles E. Gilliland.—1st ed.
p. cm.
Includes bibliographical references and index.
ISBN 978-1-60344-795-9 (book/flexbound : alk. paper)—
ISBN 1-60344-795-4 (book/flexbound : alk. paper)
1. Real property—Ownership—Texas. 2. Land use, Rural—
Texas. I. Title.
HD266.T4G55 2012
333.33′509764—dc23
                                                    2012016410

To those Texas landowners — past, present,
and to come — whose vision and management
have preserved and restored the Texas countryside
through centuries of human development

CONTENTS

ACKNOWLEDGMENTS

Many individuals contributed to the content of this book. At the outset Ivan Schmedemann blazed the trail of land market studies in Texas. In addition, a dedicated group of professionals, including James Vine, Ray Utley, Dan Daniels, Larry Kokel, Paul Bierschwale, Keith Barlow, Bill Conner, Sam Middleton, John Schneider, Dan Hatfield, and Robbie Vann, contributed important insights and suggestions.

Institutional support and encouragement came from the Real Estate Center at Texas A&M University, as well as the Farm Credit Bank of Texas.

Reviewers Charles Porter and Paul Goebel contributed many constructive comments and suggestions that improved the final volume.

Finally, my wife Diane encouraged and assisted in preparing the manuscript. She also contributed photographs for the work.

BUYING
RURAL LAND
IN TEXAS

INTRODUCTION
Achieving a Vision of Landownership

Near Comfort, the headquarters of Hillingdon Ranch, the realization of Alfred Giles's dream of carving a ranch from the wilderness. Photograph by J. P. Beato III

From farmers expanding their operations to hunters securing habitat for wildlife to environmental enthusiasts restoring native fauna on historic ranches, buyers of Texas rural land set out to transform a vision into a reality. How well the reality achieved on the ground reflects the dream depends on the owner's ability to guide activities on the land to achieve his or her design. Success in achieving such a vision requires taking numerous steps to develop an enhanced landscape that will likely have greater market appeal and a higher market value. Some owners simply desire to maintain the current landscape and hand it on to future generations. Others remake the landscape, carving roads, building dams, clearing unwanted fauna, and so forth, to enhance the land's appeal. Still others attempt to roll back conditions to an earlier time, replacing improved varieties of grass with native vegetation. An endless list of potential visions fires each individual's decision making in the context of the markets for rural Texas land.

Just as buyers' motivations and visions vary, from pure income production and capital gain to creating a particular kind of space, many obstacles threaten to derail the dreams of potential landowners. Matching the dream to the perfect site involves voyaging through a process that may have many twists and turns. Each decision in that process can alter or thwart plans. A sea of unforeseen complications can sometimes cause the cherished vision to evaporate entirely or to render a result that is a poor reflection of the buyer's goals. At each decision point in the process a buyer faces the possibility of making a mistake that will impair plans for the land. Buying land is an activity fraught with risk.

Acquiring land involves a round robin of alternately exciting and stressful activities. The search for a perfect property follows the pattern similar to a successful hunting excursion or memorable shopping spree. Wandering rural byways leads to discoveries of hidden scenic treasures or perfect platforms for agricultural production. Still, the substantial investment required to buy land means mistakes impose high costs on an unsuspecting buyer.

Finding, buying, and managing land involves not only taking on the monetary costs but also taking time away from other activities. Potential landowners thus face complicated challenges when it comes to measuring the costs they incur because they need to account for the opportunities they have forgone in order to invest the time and money needed to acquire and responsibly manage land. To assess the impact of these opportunity costs, potential buyers should begin the land acquisition process with a clear conception or vision of their goals for owning land. Whether the objectives include recreational enjoyment or raising crops and livestock or anticipated wealth expansion from appreciation or some other treasured objectives, buyers should compare the value of those anticipated benefits with the value of activities missed because of the time and effort required to make the envisioned land use a reality. For example, owning a recreational retreat may occupy a substantial block of leisure time, causing the landowner to forgo playing golf or traveling extensively. When investment returns drive land purchases, landowners must divert funds from competing investments. Buying land means that owners can invest fewer dollars in, for instance, "safe haven" government bonds; the guaranteed return of those bonds would be sacrificed, and that loss would be an opportunity cost of buying and owning land. At the outset, potential buyers should explicitly consider all of the available alternatives for achieving their goals and compare anticipated results from those alternatives to the benefits of landownership.

To anticipate and avoid possible pitfalls, potential buyers of land should arm themselves with knowledge of the phases involved in the endeavor. Information and professional guidance can help to ensure that buyers take on an appropriate or reasonable level of risk when they acquire acreage. This volume outlines the land buying process, points out potential problems, and suggests an array of resources that buyers can use to reduce the degree of risk they face in the process.

Land purchases involve four broad phases:

- Identifying desired land characteristics and property rights
- Locating a suitable property
- Estimating the value of the property
- Completing the transaction

Without taking risks, rewards seldom follow. To win the lottery, you must buy a ticket. However, the risks associated with landownership vary from one property to another. Properly executing each phase of the acquisition process allows buyers to explore the anticipated risks and rewards of landownership in a systematic way and thus identify potential stumbling blocks. For cropland and timberland investors, revenue and expense projections under different scenarios can provide a numerical guide to potential threats. Recreational user assessments rely more on subjective judgments of the impact of potential future conditions on the value of their experiences as rural landowners. This volume also seeks to help potential buyers avoid unpleasant surprises by outlining some of the major factors that can negatively impact landownership experiences.

After completing the initial phase of purchasing land (identifying desired property characteristics and property rights), buyers can turn their attention to finding a property that meets their needs, both in the immediate time horizon and in the future. The increasingly focused search narrows choices to specific regions and areas within a region. The search frequently involves a team of professionals advising the buyer in the quest for a specific property.

Following a successful purchase, new owners must adopt strategies to accomplish their plans for the land. Various programs and resources can help new owners focus their management activities for greatest effect, and careful planning can help to reduce ownership costs. This volume concludes with information on particular activities that will enhance the overall ownership experience.

Risks and Rewards of Rural Landownership

1

A field of wildflowers near Somerville. Photograph by J. P. Beato III

Responding to a presumptuous visitor who asked what the King Ranch land was worth, Robert Kleberg emphatically exclaimed, "It's not worth anything until you do something with it." That pithy reaction reveals a savvy understanding of land economics, an understanding imbued with astute insights into not only the fundamental technique of creating land value but also the determinants of land use. The King Ranch chief's astute grasp of the rewards gained by transforming current land uses to higher valued pursuits guided him in managing his family's vast holdings of South Texas rangeland. His acute management vision contributed to the burgeoning wealth of the fabled operation. Indeed, as Kleberg well knew, transferring land resources trapped in inferior uses to more highly valued activities builds fortunes while also promoting community and national development.

First and foremost, land markets serve as the playing field in a competition among potential users vying to control space. In essence, land markets are an arena where individuals settle a contest of ideas. Buyers have ideas about how to use the soils, forests, streams, and other natural resources in order to realize particular visions. Those visions may inspire plans designed to transform the land, thus reconfiguring it to serve a different purpose, which might range from an idyllic retreat to a thriving cotton field. Other potential buyers might envision a sea of rooftops. The competition among these ideas is resolved in the marketplace when winning bidders for particular land plots decide that the value of their ideas exceeds the price their rivals are willing to pay to realize their dreams.

Historical Land Use in Texas

In the Lone Star state, the marketplace for land has attracted owners with lucrative ideas, and in the context of that market one can see Texas history dramatically unfold. After all, people do not harbor abstract desires to own land. Rather, they seek control of space needed to conduct valued activities such as farming or recreation. The power to clearly envision new land-based activities drives buyers in their quest for land-ownership. The more economic value created by those land-based activities, the more an individual can afford to pay for land.

Rural land began to produce rewards when settlers transformed wilderness expanses into agricultural fields that produced crops and livestock. At first, individuals on the frontiers tamed pockets of wilderness to produce enough for their families' sustenance. Later, with careful husbanding, their land yielded a surplus that became a source of income. As the catalog of potential uses expanded in response to societal developments, benefit flows to landowners swelled, driving up land values.

In frontier times, however, as more acreage became suitable for settlement, the increasing availability of desirable land depressed land values. When Stephen F. Austin established his colony in the 1820s, settlers were flocking to Texas for its abundant, cheap land. They clearly envisioned the time when the unsettled wilderness would be transformed into an agricultural base for a thriving community. They found Texas land selling for even less than the official price of $0.125 per acre. In the United States at that time the government sold public lands into private hands for $1.25 or more per acre.

Texas enjoyed a substantial purchase price advantage in that era, but there was a catch. Austin's settlers had to carve farms out of sod-bound prairies and virgin forests in order to transform the raw, untamed expanses into assets. It was backbreaking labor. Sometimes Indians and outlaws disrupted settlers' development activities. Risk was high, but potential rewards were great for those braving the rigorous trials of frontier life. Settlers secured control of land through a validated claim to legal ownership rights eventually enforced by governments.

The first wave of modern migration to Texas was when the Spanish arrived in 1519, and other groups from foreign shores periodically swept across Texas. Each migration left impressions that persist today. Nearly three hundred years of Spanish and Mexican settlement created a symphony of melodious place-names and a chain of architectural gems that persist in the mission compounds of San José, Espada, Concepción, and San Juan, as well as the historic San Antonio de Valero, now known as the Alamo. Other ethnic groups arrived later and brought their own traditions. Anglo Americans, arriving during the period of Mexican rule, carried with them the republican principles outlined in the Magna Carta and the US Constitution. These settlers carved out of the landscape new towns that would later be known as Austin, Houston, and Dallas. German immigrants also came in large numbers and founded New Braunfels, Boerne, and Fredericksburg. Groups of Czech, Italian, Polish, and French settlers also came to use Texas land according to their unique traditions. Evidence of this social and economic development abounds in modern-day Texas maps.

For each of these settler groups, the value of the land ultimately reflected the anticipated flow of income from that land. Those income flows depended on owners' management plans gaining the greatest revenue at the lowest cost. From the heyday of settlement activities in the early nineteenth century and well into the twentieth, agriculture ruled Texas land markets as farmers and ranchers invested labor and capital on their land to produce crops and livestock. Texas thus changed from a wild frontier society to an agrarian community. Rising land prices provided evidence of this shift as Texas progressed from a rural territory to a modern state boasting twenty-five metropolitan areas following the 2010 census.

By investing capital and labor and braving substantial risks, those hardy individuals built an economy that rewarded their descendants with land valued at more than $670 per acre by 1980. According to land market studies by the Real Estate Center at Texas A&M University, this increase in land value amounts to a dramatic annual rate of return in capital gain: more than 7 percent.

By the middle of the twentieth century, economic and social changes had set the stage for a new revolution in Texas, this time in the land markets. Farmers and ranchers continued to buy land for increasingly complex agricultural production operations. However, competing buyers with diversified land use objectives began to invade even remote rural markets to promote nonagricultural activities such as hunting or birding. Not content with leasing ground for hunting and fishing, sports enthusiasts began to acquire land in order to establish sophisticated wildlife management programs. City dwellers, flush with the fruits of their own prosperity, began to seek out retreats in the countryside to escape the pressures of urban living.

Drawn by steadily rising land values, investors began to consider holding land as a potential hedge against inflation. Individuals bought rangeland not for grazing but for uses such as second homes and recreational areas. Land markets, once an exchange platform for agricultural producers, became a "trading floor" where an array of potential users competed for control of the land. Agricultural producers began competing with not only consumers who were prepared to pay well for quality recreational experiences but also investment-driven buyers holding land in order to expand their wealth. Competition among these groups severed the time-honored link between net agricultural income and land value. Land prices began to rise because they began to incorporate the value of these competing uses.

Taking Risks for Reward

Value growth stemming from social and economic development has led to arguments about the justice of enriching those who gain by simply holding land. In the late 1800s, the American economist Henry George promoted a political movement by arguing that all value increase accruing to land originated from social growth. He maintained that landowners contributed nothing to the increase in wealth created by a growing and prospering community. In his view landowners were effectively confiscating the fruits of the labors contributed by society at large, thus increasing poverty even as the economy progressed. George proposed replacing all other taxes with a single tax on land, thereby reclaiming the value society itself had created. According to George, because land was a "free gift of nature," any price demanded for it was patently unjust.

This view of land really hearkens back to more primitive times, when populations held lands in common ownership. The countryside belonged to everyone and to no one since an individual could not assert an exclusive claim to possess any particular plot. Because no individual could control access to or the use of particular locations, no one could count on capturing the fruits of their labor in using and improving land. The Native American tribes inhabiting Texas followed this approach to land use, as they had neither a tradition nor any understanding of the concept of property rights.

George's myopic view overlooks the real contributions that landowners make in the march of progress mentioned in his arguments. First, landowners maintain and develop land to make it capable of serving a highly valued use. In addition, dedicating land to a particular use prevents it from being available for other valuable uses. Those desiring to possess land are willing to bid up prices to win out over competing potential uses. Finally, George implies that landowners know for certain that they will make a profit by holding idle acreage, thus suggesting that landowners always succeed in their gamble. But what goes up sometimes comes down, and landowners face a threat of financial loss as they preserve land for an increasingly valuable use at the proper time. They face a world of uncertainty and risk their capital and management services hoping to profit in the future. Landowners lay it on the line to earn returns from current land uses until the land can support a more valuable use in the future.

Real estate professor James Graaskamp frequently reminded audiences that a person who bought land was really buying a set of assumptions about the future. At the most elemental level, those assumptions shaped the buyer's thinking during the entire decision making process, from start to finish. These basic assumptions ultimately determined how much the buyer would offer for the land. That single dollar figure—the price offered for the land—summarizes the buyer's personal judgments about anticipated benefits flowing from the set of assumptions about the future of the land. However, between the conception and creation of the envisioned use fall the shadows of unanticipated deviations from those basic assumptions.

Performance seldom matches expectations, and risk thus lurks throughout the acquisition process. For example, a farmer, anticipating adding a son to the family operation, acquires cropland, but the son chooses to pursue a career other than farming. The recreational user anticipates developing a haven for quail, but the number of quail declines, rendering that dream unfeasible. An investor, planning to convert a large tract into small ranchettes, discovers an economic downturn has diminished demand for that product. All of these situations are examples of "downside risk" in land purchases.

During the acquisition process land buyers generally strive to limit or eliminate risk. Analyzing the risk associated with the purchase of a tract of land will provide potential buyers with a list of the things that can go wrong, an assessment of the likely impact of adverse events, and estimates of the likelihood of experiencing various negative events. The potential benefits of this kind of analytical exercise depend on gaining as much information as possible about the nature of the land and its environment; with sufficient information and analysis, buyers can limit the impact of risky negative events on their plans. Well-informed buyers know that it is important to take the right risks.

MANAGEMENT RISK

Those who purchase land assume that they can use their land to pursue activities that will lead to desired ends, such as enjoying recreational experiences, generating operating income, or gaining from capital appreciation. Risk originating within the property generally arises from inappropriate expectations or mismanagement, leading to flawed operations and disappointing results. This property-related risk diminishes the rewards of landownership. For cropland owners, an analysis of the potential for disappointing results focuses on how particular features of the land may affect the anticipated income. Both location and physical features may limit possible land uses and shape future results. Whether acting as an investor who leases the land to a producer or one who personally manages the agricultural operation, cropland buyers normally forecast an anticipated income flow determined by their assumptions about characteristics of the land.

An assessment of property risk requires analysis of factors such as soil composition, water availability, access, productive features, and other characteristics that can affect costs and yields from operations. In addition, returns will also capture any change in the land's value over time. Owners must also evaluate the effects of their management on anticipated appreciation. Potential owners should define their thoughts about future operations and then estimate impacts of deviations from that envisioned ideal regimen.

Like those who purchase cropland, buyers of recreational property seek to create an ideal venue in which to pursue their envisioned activities. The quality of those activities depends on managing land to establish an environment that will optimally support recreational use. Again, the feasibility of these envisioned plans depends on the physical features of the land. An analysis of the risk for these recreational land users should examine how fully the property can support their pursuits. Finally, an effective management plan should enhance the property's appeal to future buyers and boost appreciation potential. Risk analysis for a recreational land purchase includes an honest evaluation of its potential for achieving that enhanced future value.

Investors frequently anticipate not only income from operations on the land but also substantial value growth as land use changes to more highly valued uses over time. The transition from grazing to development often contributes the major part of a return on an investment. Producers and recreational users also often anticipate upgrades in value resulting from changes in land use or increased demand for recreation. Management actions can also affect those returns, and a complete assessment of risk should rely on an analysis of trends in land markets.

Returns on investment in land, whether financial or psychological, depend on the institutional context defining the economic, social, and legal environment. Future plans for land use reflect the configuration of these external influences under current customs. This configuration of external factors is unlikely to remain constant as time passes. As the various external factors change, owners will adapt land use to address the new realities. The array of potential external influences on land use includes such things as regulations, tax policy, and societal attitudes toward land-owners.

MARKET RISK

Owner and buyer preferences can shift over time, inducing changes in returns as land use mutates to conform to new realities. An example of this type of shift would be when rising gasoline prices increase travel costs, leading potential recreational buyers to limit the distance they are willing to travel to a property. In such circumstances, a seller must find a buyer close by or lower the asking price to offset the increased transportation costs. This type of external factor effectively reduces land values. In such a situation, cropland owners, who must pay the higher prices to ship inputs like fuel and fertilizer to the farm and crops to market, face a reduced bottom line. Buyers will undoubtedly factor the increase in operating cost into any bids they submit for a property.

Changing appetites for landownership among different kinds of buyers can invalidate past management practices. Such a shift in land management practice took place across Texas as recreational users became the primary purchasers of rangeland. Prior to the advent of these consumers of land resources, ranchers had focused on producing livestock. To increase the number of animals the land could support, ranchers frequently cleared land for pastures and planted them with coastal Bermuda grass. That activity enhanced livestock production but reduced habitat supporting wildlife. When the market changed and recreational users began to dominate, the most desirable land was unimproved rangeland harboring populations of deer, quail, and turkeys. In that environment, any activity that increased livestock carrying capacity resulted in a substantial reduction in the market value of the land. Those management practices that had been prudent in the heyday of ranching were, in the new reality, activities that decreased market appeal.

CAPITAL MARKET RISK

Land markets run on borrowed money. When interest rates vary, that instability can affect land values. Restrictive lending policies that limit access to credit and drive up interest rates reduce the number of individuals who can afford to buy. A contraction of the pool of potential buyers often translates into reduced prices for land. During periods of abundant credit, lenders vie for business across the Texas landscape, with local banks actively seeking buyers and offering generous terms. For example, the Farm Credit Bank (FCB) of Texas supports landowners with available credit from its network of local associations through good times and bad. However, increasing levels of risk in credit markets can prompt the FCB to adopt more cautious lending practices.

Selling land in times of abundant credit generally presents few obstacles. However, when credit becomes more restricted, it may be necessary for the seller to finance all or part of the purchase price in order to close a deal.

POLITICAL/REGULATORY RISK

The legal framework controlling land use constantly shifts to reflect new laws and regulations affecting management. Increasingly, environmental regulations impinge on land use activities. For example, environmental regulation stemming from the Clean Water Act may prohibit previously acceptable management practices and perhaps ban activities an owner had envisioned. Another prime example of this type of risk involves the Environmental Protection Agency (EPA) and its mandate to reduce nonpoint source pollution in rivers and streams. That mandate has led the EPA to review management practices on livestock and farming operations in certain watersheds as it seeks to identify the total maximum daily loads (TMDL) of pollutants allowable in a stream under the goals set forth in the Clean Water Act. In some cases, the EPA banned particular management practices that contribute to the pollution of water flowing from private lands into streams. The Bosque River in Texas has been the target of EPA bans on some activities through a process administered by the Texas Natural Resource Conservation Commission.

Landowner rights to access and use water on private property critically affect potential land uses and thus the value of the land. Many relatively new groundwater conservation districts adopted rules that limit landowner rights to use water. Because of legal challenges to such rules, ownership rights to groundwater remain muddled in many areas of Texas. Changing rules and legal proceedings could materially affect an owner's ability to use groundwater on his or her property. Buying a property without thorough knowledge of the status of wells and district regulations affecting water use may materially affect land buyers. A buyer should make sure that any wells are properly registered with the entity controlling water usage in the area. Sometimes that authority is a groundwater conservation district. In other areas the entity may be larger, for example, the Edwards Aquifer Authority. In one instance, potential buyers inquired about the right to drill a well on property that they were in the process of purchasing. The current owner assured them that they could drill a well and pump up to twenty-five thousand gallons of water per day. That right to provide domestic water to livestock and a home on the land did not include the right to irrigate pastures and crops because the parcel of land was in the area controlled by the Edwards Aquifer Authority, where only owners with an appropriated water right were permitted to use groundwater for crop irrigation. The buyers' plans to irrigate their land were dashed because they did not understand regulations governing water withdrawal and usage in the area. Buyers must clearly understand the legal restrictions that affect water usage.

LIQUIDITY RISK

Land sales take time. When an owner needs cash, extracting funds from a land investment may take many months. The cash-strapped owner may watch helplessly as time passes and no buyer appears. Ultimately, such owners may face the prospect of selling at fire-sale prices to meet their pressing need for cash.

A buyer bent on eliminating all risk from a transaction will not find an acceptable property. Land buyers need to make peace with risk because all land acquisitions involve risk that may have a negative impact on the land's value. Buyers should strive to identify factors that may cause performance to deviate from expectations. A reasonable risk analysis examines the form and depth of possible departures from expected outcomes and their effect on ownership objectives. By anticipating possible problems, buyers may be able to eliminate or mitigate them. Learning as much as possible about the market and the property will not eliminate risk entirely, but well-informed buyers will have learned to take the right risk, one that will have the lowest likely impact on their ability to accomplish their landownership goals. To evaluate the chances of an unhappy result, land buyers should test their basic set of assumptions against available information about the land, including markets, soils, infrastructure, and community. The remainder of this book presents a guide to learning as much as possible to limit potential damage from exposure to risk.

Seeing the
End from the
Beginning

2

Front gate of a ranch near Bryan. Photograph by J. P. Beato III

Three broad aspects of ownership rest on the validity of the set of assumptions landowners make when they buy land. First, owners normally assume they have maximum control over activities pursued on their acreage. However, that assumption hinges on the bundle of property rights transferred. The content of that bundle defines the extent of an owner's control and can limit or materially affect management possibilities. Government regulations can also limit the extent of management activities. Second, buyers assume that a particular basic social and economic structure is in place and supporting their ownership goals. The potential to manage the property efficiently depends on correctly assessing the realities of this structure. Third, the future path of those social and economic forces determines the likelihood of realizing future visions of delivering the property intact (to a subsequent owner or buyer) and enhanced to function well under a future configuration of those forces. Current performance and capital gains critically depend on both the owner and property living up to these assumptions.

To avoid disappointment, a potential land owner should test each aspect of these assumptions against the realities of both the community and the market context of the land they desire to own. A systematic review of facts related to expectations following from the assumptions provides the information a buyer needs to assess the risk of deviating from foreseen results. The buyer can then use this risk analysis to devise a strategy for acquiring a property that is a good match for his or her goals for use and eventual transfer to another party.

The Need for Risk Analysis

For some owners and for particular property uses, the risk analysis may involve compiling quantitative performance measures. For example, a buyer might project crop yields over time under normal price and weather conditions to estimate income from farming activity. Deviations from projected outcomes can result from deficiencies in rainfall or changing crop prices. Actual results can exceed or fall short of projected results based on historical norms. Examining the possible array of outcomes under various combinations of the variables produces a corresponding array of potential payoffs, and the careful buyer can assume that each potential outcome has a particular chance of occurring.

This kind of risk analysis provides a potential buyer with both a worst case and a best case scenario. The buyer can anticipate the challenges presented by the worst case scenario and assess his or her ability to withstand those reversals. Further, having assembled quantitative measures to analyze competing properties, the potential buyer has thus gained insight into the relative merits of each candidate site. The assumptions about various levels of risk and potential income translate into numerically expressed expectations.

For recreational property the risk analysis might become more qualitative. An owner might foresee transforming a rugged property with poorly accessible areas into an integrated property with improved roads and the type of amenities popular in the recreational users' market. With most of the measurable return likely accumulating as capital gain, quantitative measures of the returns will likely be highly speculative. The risk analysis may thus focus on a subjective evaluation of the likelihood of achieving the envisioned improvements and transforming the property into what the owner envisioned. Failure to identify that envisioned future state might be the greatest risk for the land buyer. Because achieving the ultimate goal for the property lies far in the future, a buyer often blithely assumes things will work out well. Without a cautious acknowledgment of possible changes that may negatively impact plans for the property, the owner may fail to recognize the problems and resulting costs that such changes could generate. Plans to use a site as a hunting retreat may be thwarted when the owners of a nearby property develop the land for apartments. A country retreat for family activities may splinter family unity as heirs squabble over how to use or divide the land. For everything there is a season, including a time to sell. A wise buyer will carefully take into consideration alternative future states of the community, economy, environment, and the condition of the land. Some of these scenarios may enhance the owner's vision, while others may detract from it. The value of "seeing the end from the beginning" results from first recognizing that a risk has appeared and then having a defined strategy in place to limit the damage. Ideally, the wise buyer has envisioned various scenarios that would trigger particular actions in response to changing circumstances.

At the extreme, future conditions might be such that, in the owner's view, the costs of continued ownership outweigh the benefits. When that happens, it is time to sell. Failure to recognize conditions that will raise ownership costs could cause landowners to cling to property when conversion to cash would better suit their objectives. External conditions that might suggest the need to sell could include the appearance of non-compatible uses on neighboring tracts. Other signal conditions might relate to the owner's circumstances, such as personal health or financial reversals. An owner might even consider a particular percentage change in value as a signal that the time has arrived to sell a property. The acquisition stage is the right time to identify what eventualities should prompt a move to sell.

Devising an Exit Strategy

According to conventional wisdom, "When you aim at nothing, you will hit it." That admonition is a mirror image of ancient philosophical advice offered to travelers setting out on a journey: "Look afar and see the end from the beginning." Because the future lies at a distance, it prompts murky speculation about market conditions. Buyers often mechanically project an optimistic scenario of continuing appreciation providing handsome rewards at some nebulous point in the future. In the late 1970s real estate investment analysts routinely plugged 12 percent annual appreciation in their cash flow analyses. Asked why, they replied, "The market is going up 1 percent a month, and that is what everybody else is doing." Adopting this type of herd mentality is poor preparation for buying recreational land. Developing a plan for the eventual disposal of the land being purchased will allow a buyer to avoid the faulty assumption that the ultimate transfer of the land will somehow happen naturally.

A murky or undefined exit strategy may present the first opportunity to make a mistake in land acquisition. Most buyers know how they will use the land after they buy; many have only a vague idea about how their tenure will come to a close. Having a clear vision of the conditions that would prompt a move to end their ownership may play critically into the selection of a property at acquisition. Keeping an exit strategy in mind can help buyers to identify properties that are more likely to reach the proper state that will accomplish the goal of the defined exit strategy.

INVESTMENT LANDS

The form of an exit strategy can vary as widely as the motives inspiring land ownership. The dispassionate investor viewing land as a simple means to profit generally begins developing an exit strategy by envisioning a specific time frame for holding the property, with resale planned at a certain point in the future. This investment-oriented strategy focuses on earning cash during the holding period and anticipating an expected rate of value growth. When all goes as planned, the investor forecasts liquidation after achieving a particular gain. To justify the initial investment in the land, the owner must determine that the forecast return will exceed the next most profitable use of the capital. Often the landowner foresees selling to an end user or a developer planning a new, higher valued use for the property. The ownership transfer will occur when conditions support that higher valued use.

Seeing the end from the beginning allows investors to foresee what the outcomes will be if, in the future, the land does not sell for the expected price. Buyers of investment land can analyze expected annual cash flows under different scenarios to evaluate possible returns on the investment. Ranging from a best case scenario in which circumstances boost rents and sale prices, to a worst case set of circumstances, the risk analysis forecast provides land investors with a rational way to measure the land investment against other investment opportunities. For example, based on historical averages, a buyer may anticipate 5 percent annual appreciation. The analysis could include a forecast decline in property values as a worst case scenario resulting from unlikely negative influences in the future. When land provides a reasonable chance of achieving returns exceeding those of other investment opportunities, the investor may opt to buy property. However, even then, the analysis may argue against a purchase if the worst case results predict sizable losses. An effective risk analysis requires subjective assumptions and objective evaluation of the resulting calculations. For investors, seeing the end from the beginning may well save a potential buyer from taking the wrong risk.

This investment-driven ownership strategy differs from plans adopted by a production- or consumption-motivated landowner. These buyers' exit strategies depend on their own particular views of landownership and the function it serves in their personal lives. Given the wide variety of goals these buyers might have, the purpose of landownership might range from managing an asset in trust on behalf of a family to maintaining a personal fiefdom. Owners who have particular personal reasons for owning land should devise an exit strategy that serves their particular ownership stance.

Hunting for the perfect property can trigger a strong emotional response. In that excited state buyers risk ignoring realities that may materially alter planned results. One unavoidable reality is that landownership incurs substantial costs during the life of the investment. Another is that buyers frequently underestimate or ignore the cost of transferring land to alternate uses. Both of these realities can affect the ownership experience.

The costs of landownership include the financial sacrifice of forgoing other investment opportunities that may arise while they hold land. Property taxes, income taxes, and selling expenses all come out the owner's pocket. In addition, searching for and acquiring property generally involves a substantial investment of time and money. These sums can substantially impact the overall ownership experience.

Conversion costs can mount as an owner transforms land from one use to another. Converting pasture to cropland involves plowing and breaking up the sod and then establishing cropland conditions. In one particular case, a professional proudly acquired fifteen acres and dreamed of using it to produce a highly valued crop. Unfortunately, a tract of that size is too small to support crop production efficiently. Converting it to cropland would have been both costly and nonproductive.

FAMILY LANDS

Many Texas properties gain new owners almost by accident. Such transfers are likely the result of inadequate planning before purchase and can occur when, for example, the owner grows bored with managing chores, needs cash, or dies, leaving the undivided acreage to his or her heirs. Because of the sizable investment required to buy land, some owners end up purchasing a less expensive property that is too small for their planned use. After struggling for several years, they realize that the property can provide only an inferior recreational experience. Others purchase property believing that land is the preferred method of transferring wealth to sons and daughters. However, as one seasoned real estate counselor confided, "I thought that the best thing you could do for your kids was to accumulate land to pass on to them. You can enjoy using it, improve it, and watch its value expand over time. But after refereeing family squabbles over how to equitably divide land, I think it's the worst thing you can do. They can always divide up cash, but no one is ever happy with the division of a ranch."

Family-owned property bequeathed to a number of siblings often goes from being a unifying platform for family events to a battlefield for family conflicts. As young family members, everyone enjoyed the ranch. Hours of shared experiences created a tapestry of memories before, one by one, each child went away to school, married, and built their own homes in dif-

ferent areas. When these adult siblings finally inherit an undivided interest in the ranch, their interactions may turn into vitriolic confrontations
as differing visions for possession and use compete with those of the co-
owners. An heir living near the ranch might propose a plan to maintain
current operations. Another, facing expenses from poor health, might
prefer to cash out by selling and splitting the proceeds. Still another might
propose granting a conservation easement and adopting other practices
designed to preserve the natural character of the ranch in perpetuity.

As the sibling owners contend for control, they often see an array of
unpleasant options emerge. The brothers and sisters can hope to amicably
agree on an equal split of the acreage. However, few partition plans find
all parties agreeing to the new property lines. Positions taken by siblings
in such cases can stretch the bounds of credulity. For example, in one
case a brother insisted on a planned split granting two hundred acres to
himself while another brother and a sister shared equally in the remaining forty-five acres. He regarded the forty-five acres, which fronted on a
paved road, to be much more valuable than his hilly two hundred acres
covered with picturesque live oak trees. He steadfastly maintained that
his proposed split was a just outcome for all three owners.

His siblings disagreed, however, and a fierce confrontation ensued. In
this context, options change. Participants might agree to engage an impartial consultant to divide the ranch. After battle lines appear, though,
emotions begin to trump logic. Failing to reach an amicable agreement,
the owners can petition a Texas district court to settle the matter. In the
end, the court assumes control of the outcome. Meanwhile, the owners
likely will find that their illiquid land inheritance has become unmarket-
able because potential buyers avoid purchasing an undivided ownership.
If the court concludes that a just division of the property itself is not possible, the result likely will be a quick sale and distribution of the proceeds.
Prices in such transactions often fall below what owners anticipated. In
short, the court could impose a solution that makes none of the owners
happy. Adding to the potential for a negative outcome, this process will
likely involve legal and appraisal fees. Seeing the end from the beginning
can minimize the risk of a cherished asset becoming the focus of family
discord.

Failing to envision various future scenarios for the transfer of family
lands also means that owners may miss out on opportunities to maximize the benefits of landownership. Sometimes landowners simply do
not know "when to hold 'em, when to fold 'em." Sitting on a property

in the path of progress, they assume that the longer they hang on, the better, believing that the march of time will continue to enhance the land's marketability and drive up its value. In reality, however, real estate development trends have defined stages ranging from integration to stability to decline. In addition, when discretionary incomes decline during economic downturns, all classes of property may lose value. Sometimes the strategy of holding land in the belief that values can only rise leads owners to reject offers when land has in fact reached its maximum market appeal. Later, the owners will face diminished prospects as development has passed them by. By identifying at the time of purchase the most likely future scenario for selling the property, an owner would avoid this mistake. Before acquiring property, a well-prepared buyer will have already identified the state of development that would prompt an optimal exit from ownership of the land.

The exit from ownership could follow several defined paths, including the following activities:

- Simply sell
- Tax deferred 1031 exchange
- Develop to capture value of higher use
- Give
  - Unitrust charitable gift
  - Tax free gift
- Bequests
  - Life estates
  - Conservation easements
- Create a corporation or partnership

This menu of options indicates the potential complexity of decisions facing buyers as they embark on their search for a property. Establishing an effective exit strategy requires not only identifying land that will support an owner's desired uses but also planning an efficient transfer of ownership when the appropriate time arrives. Waiting until later to address the exit strategy may preclude choosing alternative strategies that would have produced better results had the buyer planned ahead. The planning process requires a buyer to learn about such tools as bequests, gifts, and tax deferral strategies and what steps must be followed to use them effectively.

Besides evaluating the potential benefits of using this array of legal tools, a buyer should also consider the possibility of unintended consequences resulting from various exit strategies. For example, language in the document establishing a conservation easement may prohibit children from building a home there in future years. Executing a 1031 exchange may postpone capital gains to a future date when tax rates have increased. The buyer should critically examine each strategy to identify potentially negative outcomes and evaluate the likelihood of facing those consequences. Decisions made at the stage when potential buyers are identifying the characteristics of suitable properties may affect the future value of the land and materially affect the wealth of future generations. Because of these many factors, buyers should seriously evaluate exit strategies to avoid taking the wrong risk.

Understanding Contemporary and Future Texas Land Prices

3

The rugged hills of the Trans-Pecos area. Photograph by J. P. Beato III

Seeing the end from the beginning frequently requires an owner to examine the various scenarios for future land market conditions. Will value growth create potential tax liabilities? Is value growth occurring, and is it accelerating or slowing down? Finding answers to these kinds of questions depends on having a good grasp of what makes markets tick. Historical information can provide one vital key to forming a reasonable forecast of land price dynamics. Any foray into Texas land markets should begin with a review of information about current and past market developments.

Historical Land Market Trends

Learning about land market dynamics reduces the risks inherent in buying land with a casual, laid-back approach. Being well informed does not entirely eliminate the risk of failing to match planned results, but potential buyers will at least know to anticipate possible reversals of fortune and plan accordingly. Between 1966 and 2010, rural land prices in Texas rose from $172 per acre to $2,098 per acre. In the accompanying chart showing land prices, the top of the red portion represents the nominal prices (the prices paid in the current dollars of the indicated years). Nominal price peaked at $2,247 per acre in 2008.

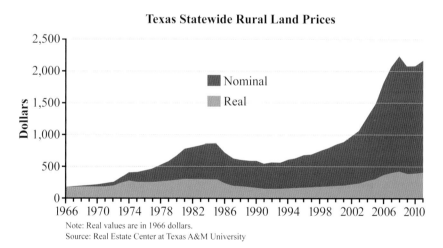

Texas Statewide Rural Land Prices

Note: Real values are in 1966 dollars.
Source: Real Estate Center at Texas A&M University

The top of the solid blue area of the chart presents "real" prices, which are nominal prices adjusted for changes in the value of money since 1966. Those constant-valued 1966 dollars provide a measure of the real change in the wealth of landowners at any given point in time. Although a current buyer will not have 1966 dollars to spend, looking at a current nominal price at its real level equivalent shows the relative amount of resources a buyer would need to divert from other uses to acquire an acre of Texas. For example, in 1966, a buyer would have forgone spending $172 on other goods to gain an acre of land. By 1973, spurred by increasing crop and livestock prices coupled with rising oil prices and migration to Texas, the nominal price swelled to $323 per acre, a roughly 88 percent increase. However, the sacrifice of $323 in 1973 equated to only $236 in 1966 currency, meaning that the purchasing power of the value gain actually increased only about 37 percent rather than the apparent 88 percent bulge suggested by the change in nominal prices. By 2008, the nominal price had ballooned to 13.06 times the 1966 price level. However, at $424 per acre, the real price had actually grown to only 2.47 times the 1966 level. That change represented a 147 percent increase in the quantity of resources needed to purchase an acre of Texas in 2008. It means that landowners in 2008 were nearly two and a half times as wealthy as their 1966 counterparts when land-based wealth is considered. Incidentally, the wealth of landowners in 2008 had grown to 180 percent of the 1973 Texas owners' land-based wealth.

This remarkable growth reflected relative levels of social and economic activities in Texas at those points in time. In general, real prices should rise as increasing population creates more competition for space. However, changes in circumstances can divert or derail social and economic progress. When that happens, real land prices mark the depth of the setback. In the 1980s, Texas suffered through a regional depression that substantially hindered economic activity. Farmers faced declining foreign demand for their output as the strengthening US dollar priced them out of international competition. Then oil prices plummeted, slowing royalty payments to trickles or stopping them entirely. Congress changed tax laws, eliminating many of the tax shelter aspects driving real estate investment. The resulting financial distress led to falling incomes and defaults on mortgages on a broad scale. Foreclosures and owners' need to raise cash led to an unanticipated swelling of the amount of land offered for sale. By 1993, at $560 per acre, Texas land prices had risen to 326 percent of 1966 prices. However, the deflated real price, at only $145 per acre, was 84 percent of the 1966 price, meaning that 1993 prices were 16 percent below the 1966 land prices. Owners had lost a substantial amount of their land-based wealth.

In fact, judging by real levels, 1993 prices were remarkably cheap compared to those of earlier years. Nominal prices reached a peak of $866 per acre in 1985 and bottomed out in 1991 at $545 per acre. Nominal prices fell about 37 percent from peak to trough, with the most dramatic declines occurring in 1986–87. Plagued by the substantial supply of lender-acquired properties for sale, real prices retreated for a couple of years more, bottoming out in 1993 at $147 per acre in 1966 prices. By then, Texas landowners had seen the value of their holdings retreat for the better part of a decade. Landed wealth measured by real prices dwindled by about 49 percent between 1985 and 1993. However, the inventory of lender-acquired properties hanging over the market was largely gone by the end of 1993. Markets then strengthened in 1994.

The ensuing years saw nominal prices post moderate and sustained increases through 2003, expanding from $605 per acre in 1994 to $1,077 per acre by 2003, a 78 percent increase in ten years. After 2003, the volume of sales began to explode, and prices likewise surged, to $2,247 per acre by 2008, a 109 percent increase in nominal prices over five years. That feverish run-up in prices boosted the 2008 real price to $424 per acre in 1966 dollars. The rate of price growth and the volume of sales during that period were both unprecedented in the recorded history of Texas land markets.

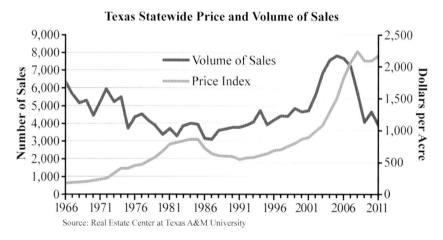

Texas Statewide Price and Volume of Sales

Source: Real Estate Center at Texas A&M University

Reviewing the history of volume of sales points to a number interesting trends. Specifically, the number of sales each year began a three-year sustained drop in 1978. Four years later, in 1982, a robust upward march in land prices faltered. Malaise set in. The drop in volume preceded a virtual flattening in nominal land prices as markets witnessed subdued sales volumes. The financial reversals of 1986–87 initiated a pronounced fall-off in activity that produced slightly more than three thousand reported sales in 1987. After the market meltdown, sales activity began to expand modestly, to levels between four thousand and five thousand transactions annually from 1993 through 2001.

Beginning in 2002 the number of land sales began to expand at an increasing annual rate. For the next two years sales volume exploded, recording 7,770 sales in 2004, more than double the 1987 low. Two years following the first spurt in volume (the 20 percent jump in 2002), size-adjusted prices registered a similar 19 percent acceleration that boomed to 23 percent growth in 2006. Participants and observers marveled at the dynamics of the market. Buyers rushed to close deals before anyone else could whisk the property out from under them. Sellers seemingly could not price land too high. The euphoria continued in 2007, as prices climbed by 14 percent, but a falling volume of sales was flashing a cautionary signal. The number of sales peaked in 2005, tapered off in 2006, and began plummeting in 2007. That plunge continued through 2009, when volumes appear to have reached levels not seen since 1990. The slow volume of sales continued into 2011.

Receding nearly 8 percent, the dramatic 2009 fall in sales volume coincided with the first significant drop in the size-adjusted price since 1991. The years following the 1991 decline saw land prices begin an expansion that would last more than a decade and lead to the rapidly escalating market of 2004. However, that 1991 dip occurred after a recent record of steadily increasing sales volumes. Following three straight years of falling volumes, the 2009 price decline erased all of the gains in nominal land prices since 2007.

Obviously, land markets respond to the underlying conditions of the broader economy. Prosperity begets appreciation, while economic setbacks tend to dampen or reverse land prices. Ample rewards await buyers acquiring land during trying times and positioning their investments in an environment likely to expand wealth as the economy recovers and expands. Many factors influence the timing of an acquisition, making the potential for capital gain one of many considerations for buyers. Although the prospect of appreciation may not be a buyer's primary aim, understanding where prices are and where they have tracked in the past helps to eliminate unpleasant surprises that could upset owner exit strategies based on unrealistic assumptions about market trends.

Table 1. Statewide trends in Texas rural land markets.

Year	NOMINAL			REAL			Volume of sales	Median tract size (acres)
	Weighted average price per acre ($)	Year-to-year percentage change	Annual compound five-year growth rate (%)	Deflated weighted average price per acre ($)*	Year-to-year percentage change	Annual compound five-year growth rate ($)		
1966	172	-	-	172	-	-	6,449	125
1967	183	6	-	177	3	-	5,695	118
1968	190	4	-	177	0	-	5,219	109
1969	200	5	-	177	0	-	5,360	101
1970	212	6	-	178	1	-	4,504	112
1971	230	8	6	184	3	1	5,290	113
1972	248	8	6	191	4	1	6,014	125
1973	323	30	11	236	23	6	5,227	157
1974	404	25	15	270	14	9	5,519	154
1975	409	1	14	250	-7	7	3,722	129
1976	440	8	14	254	2	7	4,405	131
1977	464	5	13	252	-1	6	4,566	124
1978	520	12	10	264	5	2	4,171	128
1979	582	12	8	273	3	0	3,889	135
1980	670	15	10	287	5	3	3,374	139
1981	778	16	12	305	6	4	3,721	125
1982	802	3	12	296	-3	3	3,299	106
1983	832	4	10	296	0	2	3,869	114
1984	863	4	8	296	0	2	4,037	128
1985	866	0	5	288	-3	0	3,972	119
1986	722	-17	-1	235	-18	-5	3,191	117
1987	634	-12	-5	201	-15	-7	3,077	130
1988	608	-4	-6	186	-7	-9	3,637	140
1989	594	-2	-7	175	-6	-10	3,691	140
1990	588	-1	-7	167	-5	-10	3,777	137
1991	545	-7	-5	149	-10	-9	3,780	138
1992	564	3	-2	151	1	-6	3,891	147
1993	560	-1	-2	147	-3	-5	4,109	140
1994	605	8	0	155	6	-2	4,770	132
1995	631	4	1	159	2	-1	3,929	122

Table 1. Continued

Year	NOMINAL			REAL				
	Weighted average price per acre ($)	Year-to-year percentage change	Annual compound five-year growth rate (%)	Deflated weighted average price per acre ($)*	Year-to-year percentage change	Annual compound five-year growth rate ($)	Volume of sales	Median tract size (acres)
1996	680	8	5	168	6	2	4,193	111
1997	696	2	4	169	0	2	4,428	140
1998	744	7	6	178	6	4	4,411	139
1999	788	6	5	186	4	4	4,862	120
2000	845	7	6	195	5	4	4,691	117
2001	886	5	5	200	3	4	4,721	101
2002	977	10	7	217	9	5	5,700	105
2003	1,077	10	8	235	8	6	7,000	100
2004	1,281	19	10	271	16	8	7,770	100
2005	1,487	16	12	305	12	9	8,005	100
2006	1,830	23	16	363	19	13	7,891	96
2007	2,083	14	16	402	11	13	7,344	80
2008	2,247	8	16	424	6	13	5,880	90
2009	2,083	-8	10	389	-8	7	4,139	73
2010	2,091	1	7	388	0	5	4,747	75
2011	2,170	4	3	400	3	2	4,101	74

*In 1966 dollars
Source: Real Estate Center at Texas A&M University

Searching the State

At the outset, buyers control their risk of disappointing results by making a correct, informed choice among available properties. When looking at available properties, buyers focus their search based on their intended use for the land. For a buyer interested in agricultural uses, the soils in some locations favor crop production, while other areas have soils that would better host grazing and livestock production. Conditions favoring particular uses tend to exist in regional expanses that result in clusters of similar land uses. That clustering is a product of the competitive advantage land provides within its environmental setting. For example, owners can profitably grow peaches in Hill Country orchards near Fredericksburg. If a landowner were to set out a peach orchard in the Brazos River drainage, the soils and climate would not yield a harvest to match that of the Hill Country orchards; both quantity and quality would be lower. In addition, when agricultural production surges, processing facilities follow and can profitably handle and market the output. Consequently, even if the lone Brazos orchard produces marketable quantities of peaches, the marketing infrastructure to provide profits is missing. The Fredericksburg region enjoys a competitive advantage over the Brazos bottom, where cotton and other field crops win out.

Buyers who are ready to begin their search for a property should first identify areas where their envisioned use currently dominates. Is agricultural production the primary goal? If so, are the buyers looking for irrigated cropland or do they want pastureland? What about native range or timber? Alternatively, is the primary goal to have an investment that will appreciate in value, as might land located near a growing metropolitan area? Do they want land for recreation? Some potential buyers may already have in mind an area in which to concentrate their search, while others may be more flexible at this early stage. Studying regional patterns of land use can help buyers identify areas where they are more likely to find land best suited to a particular use.

LOCATING SPECIFIC LAND TYPES

Rural land in Texas is primarily native rangeland, as the accompanying pie chart (based on reported acreages from local taxing jurisdictions) of statewide rural land use shows.

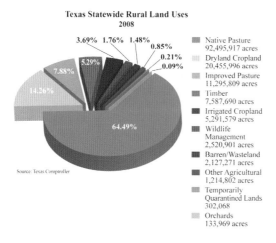

Texas Statewide Rural Land Uses
2008

3.69% 1.76% 1.48%
                    0.85%
                  0.21%
                  0.09%
5.29%
7.88%
14.26%
64.49%

Source: Texas Comptroller

- Native Pasture 92,495,917 acres
- Dryland Cropland 20,455,996 acres
- Improved Pasture 11,295,809 acres
- Timber 7,587,690 acres
- Irrigated Cropland 5,291,579 acres
- Wildlife Management 2,520,901 acres
- Barren/Wasteland 2,127,271 acres
- Other Agricultural 1,214,802 acres
- Temporarily Quarantined Lands 302,068
- Orchards 133,969 acres

According to the taxing authorities' reports for 2008, Texas rural acreage consisted mostly of grazing lands, with nearly 65 percent classified as native pasture and an additional 8 percent categorized as improved pasture. Nonirrigated cropland comprises more than 14 percent of Texas acreage. Grazing acreage and dryland cropland together make up nearly 87 percent of the total. Timber occupies 5.29 percent of Texas rural land, mostly in East Texas. At 3.69 percent of the state total, irrigated cropland is a minor land use in Texas. Nevertheless, in 2007 irrigation accounted for 60 percent of all water used statewide. Remaining categories make up less than 5 percent, and wildlife management lands in general are much like native rangeland.

REGIONAL LAND MARKETS

Texas encompasses a remarkably varied catalog of land resources. Climate ranges from the subtropical Lower Rio Grande Valley to the prairies of the South Plains and from the arid West Texas desert to the East Texas forests and Gulf Coast beaches. The accompanying map shows areas with similar land market trends. The seven designated regions reflect the collective judgment of practicing appraisers in rural Texas markets. Each region exhibits a distinct character with geographically consistent influences on land price trends.

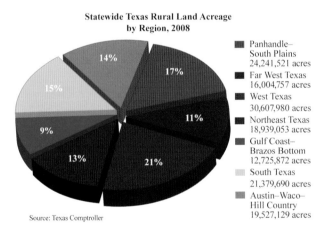

Statewide Texas Rural Land Acreage by Region, 2008

Panhandle–South Plains 24,241,521 acres
Far West Texas 16,004,757 acres
West Texas 30,607,980 acres
Northeast Texas 18,939,053 acres
Gulf Coast–Brazos Bottom 12,725,872 acres
South Texas 21,379,690 acres
Austin–Waco–Hill Country 19,527,129 acres

Source: Texas Comptroller

The West Texas (3) and Panhandle–South Plains (1) regions contain the largest acreages of the regional breakdown. The Gulf Coast–Brazos Bottom (5) has the smallest acreage region of the seven-area partition. However, measuring market activity by volume of sales paints a different picture. Although only 14 percent of the statewide rural land inventory is

Land Market Regions

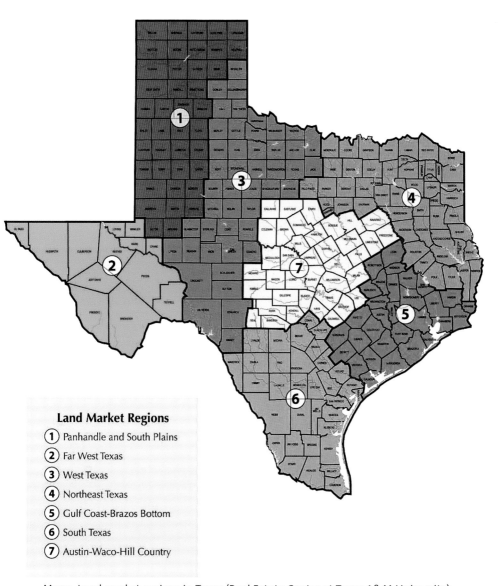

Land Market Regions

1. Panhandle and South Plains
2. Far West Texas
3. West Texas
4. Northeast Texas
5. Gulf Coast-Brazos Bottom
6. South Texas
7. Austin-Waco-Hill Country

Map 1. Land market regions in Texas (Real Estate Center at Texas A&M University).

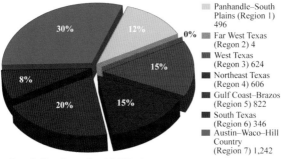

Texas Statewide Rural Land Sales Volume
Number of Sales by Region, 2009

- Panhandle–South Plains (Region 1) 496
- Far West Texas (Regon 2) 4
- West Texas (Regon 3) 624
- Northeast Texas (Regon 4) 606
- Gulf Coast–Brazos (Region 5) 822
- South Texas (Region 6) 346
- Austin–Waco–Hill Country (Region 7) 1,242

Source: Real Estate Center at Texas A&M University

located in region 7, a full 30 percent of the sales in 2009 took place in the Austin–Waco–Hill Country region, and 20 percent took place in the Gulf Coast–Brazos Bottom area. Clearly, competition for smaller inventories of land in regions 5 and 7 should and does produce higher per acre land prices than in the more sparsely populated regions 1 and 3. If a buyer is searching for the lowest price, region 1, 2, or 3 would win out over region 5 or 7.

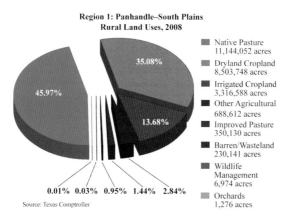

Region 1: Panhandle–South Plains
Rural Land Uses, 2008

- Native Pasture 11,144,052 acres
- Dryland Cropland 8,503,748 acres
- Irrigated Cropland 3,316,588 acres
- Other Agricultural 688,612 acres
- Improved Pasture 350,130 acres
- Barren/Wasteland 230,141 acres
- Wildlife Management 6,974 acres
- Orchards 1,276 acres

Source: Texas Comptroller

Region 1: Panhandle–South Plains. For buyers interested in low-priced agricultural land or natural landscapes, the Panhandle–South Plains offers concentrated opportunities. In this region (1) 80 percent of the land is used for dryland farming or grazing, and it contains 41 percent of the total cropland for nonirrigated production in Texas, the largest regional concentration of this land use. The irrigated cropland in the region amounts to 62 percent of the total in Texas.

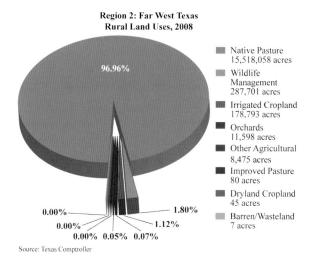

Region 2: Far West Texas
Rural Land Uses, 2008

96.96%

Native Pasture
15,518,058 acres

Wildlife
Management
287,701 acres

Irrigated Cropland
178,793 acres

Orchards
11,598 acres

Other Agricultural
8,475 acres

Improved Pasture
80 acres

Dryland Cropland
45 acres

Barren/Wasteland
7 acres

0.00%   1.80%
0.00%   1.12%
0.00%   0.05%   0.07%

Source: Texas Comptroller

Region 2: Far West Texas. For those seeking natural landscapes, Far West Texas (region 2) offers the highest mountain in Texas: Guadalupe Peak (elevation 8,749 feet). Native pasture or rangeland covers nearly 97 percent of the region. Despite being the home of El Paso, Far West Texas is the most sparsely populated area in Texas. Buyers who prize solitude can find it there.

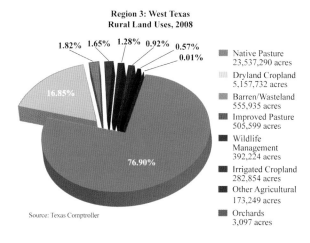

Region 3: West Texas
Rural Land Uses, 2008

1.82%   1.65%   1.28%   0.92%   0.57%
0.01%

16.85%

76.90%

Native Pasture
23,537,290 acres

Dryland Cropland
5,157,732 acres

Barren/Wasteland
555,935 acres

Improved Pasture
505,599 acres

Wildlife
Management
392,224 acres

Irrigated Cropland
282,854 acres

Other Agricultural
173,249 acres

Orchards
3,097 acres

Source: Texas Comptroller

Region 3: West Texas. The West Texas region (3), which stretches from the eastern Panhandle all the way south to the Rio Grande, encompasses 25 percent of the total native pastureland in Texas as well as 25 percent of the dryland cropland. This region offers a large expanse of open spaces.

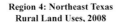

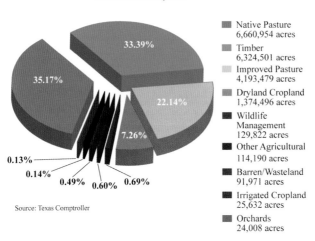

Region 4: Northeast Texas
Rural Land Uses, 2008

33.39%

35.17%

22.14%

7.26%

0.13%

0.14%

0.49% 0.60% 0.69%

Source: Texas Comptroller

Native Pasture
6,660,954 acres

Timber
6,324,501 acres

Improved Pasture
4,193,479 acres

Dryland Cropland
1,374,496 acres

Wildlife
Management
129,822 acres

Other Agricultural
114,190 acres

Barren/Wasteland
91,971 acres

Irrigated Cropland
25,632 acres

Orchards
24,008 acres

Region 4: Northeast Texas. The northeastern part of Texas (region 4) has the largest concentration of timber in the state. In terms of timber at productivity and restricted uses, this area has 86 and 88 percent, respectively, of the statewide total. Timber at productivity refers to timber slated for harvest at a future date. Restricted use timber lands are tracts where harvesting is restricted for environmental reasons.

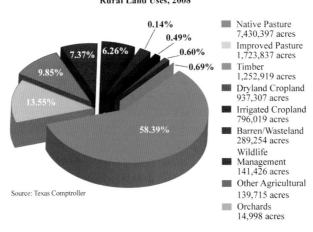

Region 5: Gulf Coast–Brazos Bottom
Rural Land Uses, 2008

0.14%

0.49%

0.60%

0.69%

7.37% 6.26%

9.85%

13.55%

58.39%

Source: Texas Comptroller

Native Pasture
7,430,397 acres

Improved Pasture
1,723,837 acres

Timber
1,252,919 acres

Dryland Cropland
937,307 acres

Irrigated Cropland
796,019 acres

Barren/Wasteland
289,254 acres

Wildlife
Management
141,426 acres

Other Agricultural
139,715 acres

Orchards
14,998 acres

Region 5: Gulf Coast–Brazos Bottom. Although native pasture predominates, with more than 58 percent of the total area, there is also considerable timber acreage (833,208 acres at productivity, 302,576 acres in timberland with a special tax status, 113,859 acres at restricted use, 3,276 acres in transition to timber). The region also contains the highly populated Houston/Galveston area, as well as Victoria, Bryan/College Station, and Beaumont/Port Arthur. With higher population density throughout the Gulf Coast–Brazos Bottom region, rural land prices are relatively high.

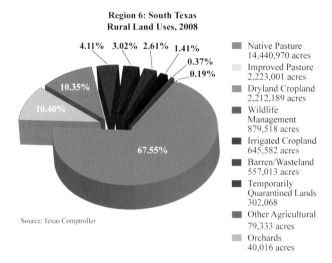

**Region 6: South Texas
Rural Land Uses, 2008**

4.11% 3.02% 2.61% 1.41%
0.37%
0.19%
10.35%
10.40%
67.55%

- Native Pasture
  14,440,970 acres
- Improved Pasture
  2,223,001 acres
- Dryland Cropland
  2,212,189 acres
- Wildlife
  Management
  879,518 acres
- Irrigated Cropland
  645,582 acres
- Barren/Wasteland
  557,013 acres
- Temporarily
  Quarantined Lands
  302,068
- Other Agricultural
  79,333 acres
- Orchards
  40,016 acres

Source: Texas Comptroller

Region 6: South Texas. South Texas (region 6) occupies an expanse of grassland once known as the Wild Horse Desert and may be of greatest interest to buyers searching for wildlife habitat, as this area has more than 34 percent of the statewide acreage devoted to wildlife management. Dryland cropland in the region amounts to 20 percent of the state total. In addition, the Rio Grande Valley subregion harbors a large concentration of orchards, with almost 30 percent of the statewide total. A large swatch of irrigated cropland flanks the lower reaches of the Rio Grande. About 1.5 percent of the region consists of lands temporarily quarantined because of an expansion of the zone designed to keep outside the area a species of tick that spreads a fatal disease to herds.

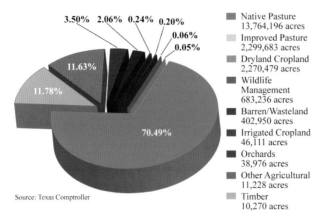

Region 7: Austin–Waco–Hill Country
Rural Land Uses, 2008

3.50%   2.06%   0.24%   0.20%
0.06%
0.05%
11.63%
11.78%
70.49%

Native Pasture
13,764,196 acres

Improved Pasture
2,299,683 acres

Dryland Cropland
2,270,479 acres

Wildlife
Management
683,236 acres

Barren/Wasteland
402,950 acres

Irrigated Cropland
46,111 acres

Orchards
38,976 acres

Other Agricultural
11,228 acres

Timber
10,270 acres

Source: Texas Comptroller

Region 7: Austin–Waco–Hill Country. Home to some of the most scenic land in the state, the Central Texas region encompassing Austin, Waco, and the Hill Country (region 7) has a heavy concentration of native pasture, 20 percent of the statewide total of improved pasture, and more than 25 percent of the statewide total for wildlife management areas. There is also a heavy concentration of orchards, with more than 29 percent of the statewide total. Timber acreage is minimal, with only 7,128 acres at productivity, 2,773 acres in transition to timber, and 369 acres at restricted use. This region also contains highly populated metropolitan areas, including Austin/Round Rock, Waco, Killeen/Fort Hood/Temple, and part of Abilene.

SIZE AND PRICE

Potential buyers who gain an understanding of markets will be better prepared to anticipate prices for specific properties. However, focusing on a median or average price may lead to a faulty forecast of future conditions for a particular type of land. Market prices vary with the size of property. Even properties with similar features sell at different prices per acre when the number of acres in each parcel is different. This price differential occurs because more potential buyers can muster the resources to compete for a small property than for a larger tract. The much larger price involved in a sizable transaction simply disqualifies most would-be buyers. Because of more spirited competition for the smaller properties, those tracts tend to sell for more per acre than comparable larger tracts. For example, a three-hundred-acre ranch property might sell for fifteen hundred dollars per acre, while a property with similar characteristics in a fifty-acre tract commands a price of twenty-five hundred dollars per acre in the same market. Market prices tend to vary inversely to expanded property size; the larger the property, the lower the per-acre price. Because of this situation, studies of trends in land prices based on sales should always include an analysis of how size influences price per acre. Studying land market trends of prices divided into size-defined segments provides an understanding of the relative price per acre for properties of various sizes within a region.

Each land market segment can be related to all other segments in the region to provide a potential buyer with an understanding of per-acre prices for properties of differing size. For example, a median price in sales of properties smaller than fifty acres in the Hill Country might mislead a buyer considering acquiring a hundred-acre tract. Researching size variations might suggest that the price of a one-hundred-acre tract should typically be about 53 percent less than the small property price when all else is equal.

From 2005 through 2009, Texas regional land markets posted prices reflecting the size-related adjustments to median prices shown in the accompanying table. The information in the body of the table indicates the adjustment to prices for the combination of sizes listed in the left-hand column and top line of each table. The table can be read vertically or horizontally. For example, in the Panhandle and South Plains, the price of a property smaller than 160 acres would require a negative 24 percent adjustment for property prices posted in the 161–180 acre range. A price of $1,000 in the segment for parcels of less than 160 acres would indicate a price of $760 per acre in the 101–180 acre segment ($1,000 minus $240). These tabular data provide a general guide to the relative price adjustments observed in these markets over the years from 2005 to 2009.

For example, the Austin–Waco–Hill Country region (7) is dominated by rangeland prized for its scenic characteristics and substantial expanses of cropland and pasture. Expanding urban populations in the region have prompted landowners to subdivide large holdings, resulting in a sizable volume of relatively small sales. An analysis of region 7 sales over a forty-two-year period indicates substantial variation in prices based on the size of the acreage. The median price for the third-class size (96–155 acres) in the middle of the distribution was $762.50 per acre over the forty-two-year interval. The median price for the smallest tracts (less than 50 acres) was $1,231.25 over the forty-two years. These figures suggest that small

Table 2. Percentage price adjustments for regional land market segments, 2005–2009.

PANHANDLE AND SOUTH PLAINS

Size (acres)	< 160	161–180	181–320	321–550	> 550
< 160	0	32	20	37	30
161–180	-24	0	-9	4	-1
181–320	-17	10	0	14	8
321–550	-27	-4	-12	0	-5
> 550	-23	1	-8	5	0

FAR WEST TEXAS

Size (acres)	500–8,000	> 8,001
500–8,000	0	39
> 8,001	-28	0

WEST TEXAS

Size (acres)	< 95	96–160	161–240	241–500	> 501
< 95	0	50	87	85	99
96–160	-33	0	24	23	32
161–240	-46	-19	0	-1	7
241–500	-46	-19	1	0	7
> 501	-50	-24	-6	-7	0

Northeast Texas

Size (acres)	< 34	35–54	55–88	89–157	> 158
< 34	0	64	86	118	168
35–54	-39	0	13	33	63
55–88	-46	-12	0	18	44
89–157	-54	-25	-15	0	22
> 158	-63	-39	-31	-18	0

GULF COAST–BRAZOS BOTTOM

Size (acres)	< 43	44–67	68–100	101–181	> 182
< 43	0	53	75	121	182
44–67	-35	0	14	44	84
68–100	-43	-13	0	26	61
101–181	-55	-31	-21	0	28
> 182	-65	-46	-38	-22	0

SOUTH TEXAS

Size (acres)	< 45	46–90	91–165	166–365	> 366
< 45	0	84	114	157	189
46–90	-46	0	17	40	57

Table 2. Continued

SOUTH TEXAS (CONTINUED)

91–165	-53	-14	0	20	35
166–365	-61	-29	-17	0	12
> 366	-65	-36	-26	-11	0

AUSTIN–WACO–HILL COUNTRY

Size (acres)	< 50	51–95	96–155	156–280	> 281
< 50	0	79	111	138	148
51–95	-44	0	18	33	39
96–155	-53	-15	0	13	18
156–280	-58	-25	-12	0	4
> 281	-60	-28	-15	-4	0

properties in region 7 historically sold for 161.5 percent of prices registered for land in the middle-size interval, a 61.5 percent premium. In the 2005–2009 analysis in the table above, the premium for the small property segment had expanded to 111 percent for the 96–155 acre category.

The largest tracts (more than 281 acres) in the forty-two-year study, with a median price of $576 per acre, sold at 75.5 percent of the middle interval median price, a 24.5 percent discount from prices in the 96–155 acre class. As an updated analysis of the 2005–2009 period shown in table 2 indicates, that discount had narrowed to only 15 percent in that five-year interval. In the forty-two-year analysis, the 156–280 acres class reflected a 13.9 percent discount, while the 51–95 acres class registered a 21.0 percent premium in per-acre price. The 2005–2009 results showed a 12 percent discount and 18 percent premium, respectively.

These analyses indicate that variations in property size do impact price trend indicators in Texas land markets. The amount of premium and discount varies across the different areas of Texas and appears to vary in magnitude as markets change with the times. Land buyers studying the market prospects of particular properties need to develop an appreciation of the dynamics of prices over time and market segments to make informed estimates when setting parameters for their exit strategies.

By studying trends in prices, the prospective buyer can evaluate current land market realities in comparison with past performance. Placing current conditions in historical context allows buyers to not only make judgments about current asking prices but also anticipate the direction of future trends. The prudent buyer should forecast likely prices at various points in the future. Knowledge of the size-related discount or premium will allow a prospective buyer to adjust those price forecasts to conform to the size of the targeted property.

Knowledge of size premiums for small tracts may also help prospective buyers develop good exit strategies. By anticipating higher per-acre prices for small properties, owners may opt to split larger holdings to appeal to more potential buyers. However, a smaller number of wealthy buyers may seek large holdings. Such buyers sometimes pay premium prices for contiguous large properties. These influences tend to ebb and flow with changes in economic conditions.

Finding That Perfect Spot

4

An East Texas landowner advertises the intent to sell.
Photograph by J. P. Beato III

Between 1970 and 2000 the timber industry changed considerably. Concentrating on controlling the supply of product, major timber companies had acquired vast tracts in all forested parts of the United States. However, the corporate tax structure and booming investment returns in other areas vastly increased the opportunity cost of holding land. The major timber companies could earn more by investing their capital in other assets than they could by holding land. One by one the big companies sold their land holdings until the last holdout, Temple-Inland, finally capitulated and sold its timberland holdings. While that monumental sale was in progress, one lucky buyer discovered that he could secure a particular three-hundred-plus–acre stand of pines to call his own. In his zeal to buy, he checked overall price levels but paid scant attention to prices recorded on nearby properties. The deal closed without a hitch, and the buyer took title to the land. The company retained the timber but would not harvest it for years. The company also kept the mineral rights and lignite, but the buyer was not interested in those details; all he wanted was to use the land for his enjoyment and maybe make a little return grazing a few cows. He never realized that skipping the step of identifying the physical characteristics and property rights made his buy a risky proposition.

After taking possession, he gated both ends of a road crossing the property and prepared to enjoy his land. Then things began to go wrong. First, the road happened to be a dedicated county road, so the gates across it had to be left open, permanently. Next, he discovered the company's timber rights banned any use that might impact timber growth, so no cows could graze the land. Suddenly, the dream buy turned disappointing. Shortcutting a measured acquisition process in a frenzied rush to buy before someone else snatched up the acreage had caused him to buy less than he had assumed he would own. He bought in a hurry but repented in leisure. The surprises followed from neglecting to follow a methodical process designed to analyze the suitability of the land for specific plans and to reduce the risk of an unsatisfactory outcome.

A land purchase represents a sizable investment, so before rushing to sign a deal potential buyers should adopt an orderly approach to evaluating the risks associated with each candidate property. Armed with an understanding of basic land market trends, a buyer can press on in earnest with the acquisition process. Buyers should review their explicit reasons for purchasing land so as to accomplish their previously articulated plans for use and ultimate transfer of the land. The next phase focuses on systematically evaluating characteristics of candidate properties that may pose a risk to their plans. That evaluation guides the buyer's quest by offering a defined set of steps designed to examine all important aspects of the property. Buyers typically follow a similar pattern in approaching the purchase. Some thoroughly develop each step, while others skip over or ignore steps, believing that matters will work out to reach a satisfactory result. Nevertheless, even those buyers confident in their less detailed approach tend to follow a variation of the following programmed steps:

- Identifying and evaluating relevant physical attributes of candidate properties: walking the land and noting elevations, vegetation, available water, roads, fences, and improvements
- Identifying and studying local economic trends likely to affect property values
- Establishing and evaluating the extent of current ownership rights and identifying limitations on the seller's ownership, such as water rights, existing leases, easements, and any other entities with a potential ownership claim
- Identifying the character of nearby communities, estimating their impact on property owners, and investigating school board, county, groundwater conservation district, municipal, and other special district policies that might impact landowners

Deliberately and thoughtfully following these steps will lead buyers to explicitly recognize all important assumptions they may make during the acquisition process. Because of the diversity of natural resources across Texas, the set of assumptions about future land uses can differ immensely from one location to another. Because the purchase involves substantial nonrecoverable costs, buyers should embark on the process with a thoroughly prepared plan to reduce the chances of taking the wrong risk.

Useful Sources for Property Searches

A review of regional land uses and land market developments should help a potential buyer identify likely areas in which to search for the perfect place. Buyers often choose a location based on personal experience. They know that they want to be in the Hill Country or near the coast or perhaps Far West Texas. The review of regional statistics described in the previous chapter may confirm those desires or perhaps lead to consideration of an entirely different locale. Once a general region becomes a search candidate, the process of identifying prospective properties comes into focus. Investigating specific properties can involve substantial costs when a buyer sets out to find properties offered in various areas. Traveling through those regions, the buyer can read local newspapers, keep an eye peeled for posted "For Sale" signs, or even knock on doors and ask. This on-the-ground approach may produce satisfactory results, but a prospective buyer can enlist various tools to save time and increase the likelihood of a positive result. Using various proven tools and depending on professional assistance can substantially reduce search costs and lessen the risk of encountering unanticipated problems.

REAL ESTATE BROKERS AND LICENSEES

Licensed real estate agents specializing in rural properties constantly monitor market developments in specific areas. Many belong to professional associations that conduct marketing sessions on a regular schedule, and many subscribe to listing services that offer broad public access to properties offered for sale. Engaging the services of an informed and effective agent can reduce search costs. In addition, these agents frequently know the history and market experience of a vast array of properties in their market area. These seasoned agents may also know about properties not yet for sale that meet the buyer's criteria. In addition, they often do not shrink from asking an owner to consider selling. Drawing on that body of knowledge can help both buyers and sellers to conclude an efficient transaction.

Many agents specializing in selling land join professional associations designed to assist them and their clients in marketing properties. These affiliations underscore agents' commitments to the real estate profession and their close ties with those who share a professional interest in rural land markets. The associations range from rather informal groups that maintain contacts and listings to formal professional associations providing educational support and an affiliation with parent national organizations. Many professional real estate agents participate in more than one of these organizations. Some of the most active professional organizations in Texas are the following:

- *Realtors Land Institute (RLI)*. RLI members belong to the Texas chapter of the national affiliate of the National Association of Realtors. RLI supports its members by offering an educational program designed to enhance their professional skills. That program can lead to the member earning recognition as an accredited land consultant after completing the educational program known as the Land University. See http://www.rliland.com/AboutRLI.aspx.

- *Texas Alliance of Land Brokers (TALB).* Members of the TALB focus on all types of land in Texas. The association has no national affiliation, but many members also belong to other professional groups. The group meets periodically to exchange information and participate in educational programs. The group's primary function lies in networking and providing an avenue for publicizing listings on a website. See http://www.texaslandbrokers.org/index.php.

Agents frequently represent sellers in the transaction process. However, many brokers and licensees also represent buyers and advise them in their quest for landownership. Buyers may find it very helpful to engage the services of one of these professionals. Some of these agents can actually ferret out properties that are not on the market and persuade the owner to sell. Engaging their services can ease the burden of searching out the ideal property.

REAL ESTATE APPRAISERS

First and foremost, appraisers know value. They constantly monitor economic and societal changes that enhance or erode land values. Appraisers routinely maintain files filled with information about transactions in local markets where they practice. They know the trends and the property values in their communities of interest. In addition to having an appraiser's license, many rural property appraisers also maintain a real estate broker's license. They serve as both appraisers and agents in the rural land market. Because they specialize in knowing the conditions that enhance value, they also often serve as advisors for land buyers and landowners.

Some rural appraisers belong to both RLI and TALB. In addition, many join other professional associations that concentrate on appraisal. The following list represents perhaps the foremost organizations for rural property appraisers:

- *American Society of Farm Managers and Rural Appraisers (ASFMRA).* ASFMRA members belong to a national organization with state-level chapters. Members typically specialize in either professional farm management or appraisal. The society supports these members by maintaining an ambitious educational program in each discipline and certifying members who successfully complete course work and demonstrate practical professional competence. Appraisers meeting ASFMRA requirements earn the Accredited Rural Appraiser (ARA) designation. ASFMRA also maintains a continuing education program for members. Those earning and maintaining an ARA designation are recognized specialists in rural and agricultural property appraisal. See http://www.ASFMRA.org.

- *Appraisal Institute.* Perhaps the most recognized professional appraisal organization in the United States, the institute supports its members with a comprehensive and intensive educational program. Those members who complete the program and demonstrate a specific level of appraisal expertise earn the Member of the Appraisal Institute (MAI) designation. Many MAIs concentrate on primarily urban-related assignments. However, some members do work in rural land appraisal and consulting. An increasing number of MAIs also are obtaining the ARA designation. See http://www.appraisalinstitute.org/.

LENDERS

Lenders have unique insights into the economic life of the communities they serve. Often, they have advance notice of landowners' plans to sell their properties, and they may also know when a landowner is facing financial difficulties. In addition, they attempt to monitor trends in land prices to gauge the strength of potential collateral for loans. Member associations of the Farm Credit Bank deal extensively with rural Texas. In many areas, local commercial banks also do business in land markets. See http://www.farmcreditbank.com/default.aspx.

ATTORNEYS AND TITLE COMPANIES

Most land transactions close under the watchful eyes of an attorney and/or title company representative. The legal documents used in a real estate transaction normally require specialized knowledge to ensure that the transaction accomplishes the goals of buyer and seller in transferring the property. As participants in the closing, attorneys and title company representatives must know the financial details of the transaction. However, many of the details may be proprietary. Nevertheless, attorneys and title company representatives often can quickly provide vital nonconfidential information about markets and properties. Attorneys may also have insights into properties that are not formally on the market but that could be purchased.

Appraisal districts keep track of landownership and prices in their mission to value all properties for property taxes. Although Texas does not require buyers or sellers to report prices, most appraisal districts have established methods of obtaining such information. In the process, the districts maintain a set of ownership maps showing property boundaries and records that describe property improvements. These records frequently include photographs and evaluations of the physical condition of buildings. In addition, district appraisers generally review properties periodically and may have knowledge about particular sites and their history. Although privacy concerns prohibit districts from making all of their information available online, a buyer often can find much useful information at district websites. For a comprehensive list of appraisal districts in Texas, see http://taad.org/cad_web_links.html.

THE INTERNET

The Internet has revolutionized land marketing by literally displaying offered properties to the world. Many professional land brokers maintain websites with descriptive listings for their offerings. In addition, RLI and TALB offer listing services to their members. However, perhaps the most comprehensive marketing platforms offering access to buyers, sellers, and agents are the following:

- *Lands of Texas.* One of the most popular sites for listing available properties, the Lands of Texas website allows users to search for listed properties meeting their specified criteria. In addition to conducting searches among currently listed properties, users can sign up for alerts delivered by e-mail when properties meeting their specifications come on the market. In the Wants & Needs section, users can post a request for property, including requests for leases and specific property rights. Since its inception, this site has developed into an invaluable tool for buyers and sellers alike and is widely used by real estate agents. The site contains a listing of member agents, and most of those agents include links to their individual websites. See http://www.landsoftexas.com/texas/index.cfm.

- *Multiple Listing Service (MLS).* Local associations of realtors frequently maintain multiple listing services that indicate what properties their members are currently offering. Much of the information the MLS offers focuses on residential sales, but in some areas the service also includes rural land. MLS offerings of rural land are most likely to include land in transition from open space status to development or pre-development. In some areas the MLS is a source of information for rural land markets. Frequently, the MLS places this information on the Internet.

LAND MARKET PUBLICATIONS

A growing number of publications, offered in print and online, present listings of Texas ranches for sale. The most prominent ones, some of which have nationwide listings, are the following:

- *Lands of Texas Magazine,* http://www.landsoftexasmagazine.com
- *Farm and Ranch,* http://www.farmandranch.com/home.htm
- *LandReport,* http://www.landreport.com/
- *Open Fences,* http://www.openfences.com/

Local newspapers may also be very useful sources of information.

"FOR SALE" SIGNS

A low-tech alternative to the electronic trading platform is the lowly "For Sale" sign. Most brokers place a sign with contact information on the property. Cruising country roads may be an enjoyable experience leading to the perfect place.

Identifying Suitable Properties

The many useful sources of information on rural properties will help a potential buyer track down likely prospects. Buyers can begin their evaluation process with this information, but choosing candidate properties and narrowing the search to one winner is an inherently risky task. Gathering information helps the buyer evaluate the physical features defining each site and then judge how those features impact the property's potential to fulfill their planned uses. Evaluating the physical attributes leads buyers through the first rigorous examination of their assumptions about the future that will follow from those characteristics.

Buyers must not, however, rely solely on documentary information when evaluating a property. Internet information, sales brochures, maps, and photographs do not convey all of the necessary details. Property features include not only length and width but also elevations and depressions that can create stunning vistas or disappointing eyesores. Buying a rural property secures owner access to not only its hills and valleys but its rocks and holes. The potential buyer must walk the land to evaluate all of its features, including those that may not be the type of feature that attracts attention. Before walking the land, a buyer should prepare a list of the characteristics of particular importance in his or her plan for the property and be prepared to check off each item during the tour. On the first trip to each candidate property, a buyer should also evaluate the appearance of the land and the approach to the front gate. For example, a buyer should observe:

- Road widths and construction
- Bar ditches
- Road and entrance overhangs
- Blind curves and approaches
- Sight lines
- Overhead utilities
- Gate and bridge widths
- Cattle guards

From ease of access to the aesthetic appeal of the entrance, a prospective purchaser should evaluate the approach to each candidate property with an eye to currently planned uses and future disposal strategies. One East Texas landowner confessed that when he conducted his property search, he had paid little attention to potential access issues; he approached his candidate property along an unpaved dirt road through a picturesque tunnel of pine trees. After he bought the land, the neighboring landowner closed the lane, cutting off access to the newly acquired property. With no access through neighboring properties, the new owner suffered a substantial loss and was forced to seek expensive remedies in a futile attempt to establish access.

Another owner found an attractive property at the end of a lane that meandered past a line of dilapidated mobile homes. In the frenzied market of the day, he bought the land quickly, without thinking about the unattractive approach. However, when markets cooled, potential buyers found an abundant inventory of competing sites and shied away from his land. It became difficult to attract prospective buyers even to view the land. The lesson here is that, when possible, a buyer should strive to find and be willing to pay extra for land with attractive features. The more appealing the property, the more marketable it will be in the future.

Another physical feature to which buyers should be alert is a railroad track along the property line. Railroads jealously guard access to their tracks. Negotiations regarding track crossings take place on the railroad's terms if they occur at all. Buyers should not hesitate to ask questions and investigate potential problems in approaching the land. Access should be secure and free of nuisances. Superior access characteristics enhance prospects for the future of a property.

One land investor tersely observed, "I never knew anyone who made money by buying junk." Junk comes in many forms, but appearance creates a first impression or initial judgment about a property. With their future exit strategy in mind, buyers should judge properties in the present based on the assumption that they might someday sell the land. Thus, when a buyer sees a property with a family dump tucked away in a gully, it not only presents the ugly appearance of clutter but also leads to speculation on the nature of items disposed there. Perhaps discarded containers spilled toxic substances into the soil. If that were the case, legal or environmental concerns might preclude future alternative uses for the land or an owner might incur significant costs to clean up problems created by prior activities. Pesticides, asbestos, fuels, toxic or hazardous wastes, and other problematic substances deposited on the site transfer substantive liabilities to the new owner once title has passed.

A large-scale example of prior activities precluding future alternative uses and thus canceling a land transfer occurred when Texas A&M University turned down a proposed donation of land in East Texas where the Pershing missile had been tested. The land fronted on Caddo Lake for more than a mile, with thousands of acres of pine and hardwood forests crisscrossed by paved roads and railroad tracks. The property also boasted numerous buildings. However, the buildings contained asbestos, and a substantial number of the trees were riddled with bits of metal, rendering them useless as timber. In addition, toxic waste had seeped into the groundwater. The site was more of a liability than an asset.

Composition of soils has a significant impact on potential uses of rural land. Buyers should examine the soil to identify its characteristics and evaluate its suitability for their planned management strategies. A farmer who moved south to the Lower Rio Grande Valley saw the black lands north of the town of Mercedes and equated them to the fertile black soil bottomland in his former home. He later discovered to his dismay that the black soil in the mid-Valley was not especially fertile and thus offered poor farming opportunities.

In addition to presenting agricultural limitations, soils may suffer shortcomings from an engineering perspective and be unsuitable for particular uses. For example, heavy clay soils may expand and contract with changes in moisture levels, making them poor candidates for buildings with concrete slab foundations. Homeowners given to black humor in the blacklands prairie area of Texas claim that the dry summer months cause soils to shift, opening cracks in the walls of houses to improve ventilation, and, in winter, the rains swell the soil and close up the fissures, keeping the cold at bay. Buyers should be prepared to identify the kinds of soils found on a property and investigate their suitability for various uses. (See chapter 5 for information on using maps to assess soils at candidate sites.)

Improvements can enhance the value of a property or reduce its appeal. The effect depends on the kind of improvements made and their condition when the property is on the market. Sturdy, useful barns and pens add to property value. Because buildings designed for agricultural purposes seldom can be adapted to an alternative use, an abandoned poultry house, for example, may actually reduce property value. A buyer should inspect existing buildings, fences, pens, and the like to ascertain their physical condition as well as their effective ability to contribute to property operations.

The presence and extent of utilities can enhance property value by establishing the possibility of transforming the land to a higher valued use. Potential buyers should determine if potable water is available, if there is a sewer line close by, and what kind of electrical service there is and if it is reliable. Thus, the buyer must know in advance if existing utilities will support planned uses. For example, if a buyer wants to set up a modern dairy operation, the land must have access to three-phase electricity. Land located at a distance from available three-phase power will not be a candidate for a dairy operation without the owner spending considerable sums to bring that utility service to the tract. Land without access to sewer and water service also suffers a disadvantage compared to sites that have those amenities. The lack of ready access to utilities may disqualify a site or imply added expense compared to a similar property that does have that access.

The availability of water has historically guided many decisions about how to use land. Arid environments require irrigation to make the soil productive. Subtropical locations need adequate drainage to avoid accumulating brackish pools that will incubate voracious mosquitoes. Ranchers must water livestock, and cattle prefer a short trip to available drinking water. A ranch without properly spaced watering spots suffers in comparison to one with adequate water supplies. The buyer should determine the presence and availability of both groundwater and surface flows available from rivers and lakes. The physical presence of water does not ensure its availability, however, as will be discussed later in relation to the legal right to use available supplies. However, the water must be present before the right to use it assumes any importance.

Buyers should ascertain the physical quantity of available water, but it is equally important that they also evaluate the quality of water at the site. A buyer planning to develop a grove of avocado trees in the Lower Rio Grande Valley might choose to locate at the southernmost site available, so as to reduce the probability of suffering a destructive freeze. However, avocado trees are sensitive to dissolved salts in irrigation water. Unfortunately, available irrigation water downriver from Brownsville can frequently contain dissolved solids exceeding amounts tolerated by avocado trees. Careful evaluation of the conditions needed for growing avocados reduces the risk of crop failure.

The catalog of desirable physical characteristics the buyer articulates will establish the defining set of assumptions about land use that guides the search. Those attributes become a scorecard of sorts as the search for candidate properties proceeds. The buyer begins to understand exactly what to look for in the quest for acreage. Some of the points can become "deal killers," depending on the buyer's attitude toward changing planned uses or the expense that would have to be undertaken to correct a perceived inadequacy. The buyer should investigate all of the following attributes of candidate properties:

- Appearance
- Soils
- Utilities
- Water
- History of use

Evaluating Physical Attributes

5

The Guadalupe River in Kerr County. Photograph by Gary Maler

Because location plays a pivotal role in generating enjoyment and profit from land use, available mapping software sites provide valuable insights into access, appearance, improvements, and surface water on candidate properties. Buyers can find various mapping resources to examine features of candidate properties. Websites like those in the list that follows provide detailed maps of all locations in Texas:

- Google Earth, http://www.earth.google.com/
- Bing Maps, http://www.bing.com/maps/?FORM=Z9LH7
- USDA Farm Service Agency (historical and current aerial photographs), http://www.fsa.usda.gov/
- Texas Association of Appraisal Districts, http://www.taad .org/cad_web_links.html
- MapQuest, http://www.mapquest.com/
- Yahoo Maps, http://www.maps.yahoo.com/
- Google Maps, http://www.maps.google.com/
- US Geological Survey, http://www.usgs.gov/pubprod/

Each service offers an abundance of features designed to present many attributes of particular property locations. Some of the sites provide the geographic longitude and latitude coordinates for use in other geographic information system (GIS) applications. All offer aerial photographic maps. Buyers should easily be able to find candidate properties by becoming acquainted with one or more of these sites.

Texas AgriLife Extension Service

The Texas AgriLife Extension Service (http://agrilifeextension.tamu .edu) provides valuable information to landowners and the general public throughout Texas. County agents, one located in each county, have knowledge of local properties and sources of information. They can direct potential buyers to agencies or individuals with critical knowledge about land in the area. They also can provide estimates of costs and returns for various land uses. The search for a suitable property should involve a visit to the county agent early in the process. Buyers will find them to be very helpful in the location process and with management issues after a purchase.

Farm Service Agency

Operating under the US Department of Agriculture, the Farm Service Agency (FSA) acts as the local interface between the USDA and local farmers. The FSA maintains records on farms participating in an array of programs ranging from crop price support and crop insurance to conservation. It also provides loans and loan guarantees. To accomplish its various missions, the FSA maintains information on farms participating in their programs. They also maintain a set of detailed, recent aerial maps. Potential owners can secure much information by contacting the FSA office in their area.

Web Soil Survey (WSS)

Soil surveys for most locations in the country come from the Natural Resource Conservation Service (NRCS) of the US Department of Agriculture. The surveys provide a wealth of specific information on the soil properties at specified locations. The data provide a thorough description of the soil characteristics of each surveyed property. Farmers, ranchers, engineers, developers, land use planners, park and recreational area planners, appraisers, homebuyers, and homeowners could all benefit from using soil survey data when evaluating plans for particular sites.

For example, a buyer planning a farming operation can use the data to identify potential crops for the land and to estimate the expected yields. Ranchers can use the data to gain insights into the numbers of animals they can comfortably graze, as well as the potential for making hay. A buyer planning a rural home can evaluate potential locations on candidate sites. Some soils will support foundations on slabs while others will not. Engineers and developers can find information on depth of soil, shrink-swell properties, wetness, erodibility, flood hazards, and slope to determine the development potential of the property. The service is comprehensive, and it is free. Soil surveys are online at the Web Soil Survey (WSS) website, http://websoilsurvey.nrcs.usda.gov.

Such a comprehensive database offers a challenge for those seeking to access the information. However, each soil map on the site identifies in rich detail the different soil types found in the mapped area. Therefore, a potential buyer should make an effort to use this invaluable tool. Because it can be difficult to access, this description is designed to lead a beginner through the process of accessing the soil maps.

In addition to photo maps, the WSS site contains volumes of information explaining the terms used in and concepts underlying the survey. Accessing that information is done in three steps: first, identifying a property; second, viewing the soil maps and data related to that property; and, finally, creating a customized report. The following description outlines steps to access specific soil survey information and provides a detailed guide to effective use of the site. It would be useful to access the WSS on the Internet and outline an example site while reading this guide.

Recent notifications from the Lands of Texas website indicated that the asking price for a particular property had been substantially reduced. The property information displayed an attractive photograph of pine trees on the East Texas tract. The new price weighed in at approximately one thousand dollars per acre, an attractive price for the area. The notice included information that the site contained considerable marshland. Finding the tract on WSS and outlining it revealed that approximately two-thirds of the acreage was indeed wetland. The pine trees occupied a small portion of the tract. WSS data indicated that part of the tract had areas suitable for building, but most of the property was not suitable for that use. In fact, WSS maps showed the wetland areas with a red overlay indicating severe limitations for virtually all investigated uses. WSS could have saved a potential owner a trip to investigate the property if those restrictions foiled planned uses.

Access the website http://websoilsurvey.nrcs.usda.gov/app/ and check for your system's compatibility with the program. Then click the Start WSS button and begin to define an area of interest (AOI) that specifies the geographic boundaries of the target property. Use the Quick Navigation panel (on the left) and/or the Interactive Map panel (on the right) to accomplish this step. One quick way to start is to begin using Quick Navigation to view a particular state and county, and then zoom in on the Interactive Map to highlight a specific tract.

After zeroing in on the property, click one of the two AOI tabs at the top of the map. This area of interest tool outlines the boundaries of the property. One AOI tool outlines a rectangle. Use the other AOI tab to access the polygon tool to outline irregularly shaped properties. The polygon AOI tool allows the user to point to property corners with the cursor. At each corner, a click of the mouse fixes that corner of the boundary. Proceeding to the next corner and repeating the click results in a heavy red line between the two points. Continuing around the perimeter of the property produces a heavy red outline of the property. After returning to the starting point, double click the mouse and the perimeter is set. Clicking on the Soil Map tab clips the soil map files for the defined area, displaying a list of soil types found on the property. Clipping the soils can take some time. This soil map can be printed or added to a custom report.

To access information about the soil types in the AOI, select the Soil Data Explorer tab. This tab provides access to the Suitabilities and Limitations for Use tab, the Soil Properties and Qualities tab, and the Ecological Assessment tab. The associated pull-down menus offer an abundance of information on soil characteristics affecting possible land uses. The Intro to Soils tab provides substantial amounts of information about the soil science underlying the work of the survey.

The Suitabilities and Limitations for Use tab describes the soil's characteristics in the categories of

• Building site development
• Disaster recovery planning
• Land classifications
• Land management
• Vegetative productivity
• Water and waste management

The Soil Properties and Qualities tab details

• Soil chemical properties
• Soil erosion factors
• Soil physical properties
• Soil qualities and features
• Water features

If the soil survey database includes data on a particular soil property for the AOI, the system provides a description rating for the soils.

Farmers and ranchers will likely focus on vegetative productivity to determine expected yields of irrigated crops or range forage. Reports detail crop yields in bushels or pounds of forage that specific soils can produce. Other potential buyers might opt to view the data under the Wildlife Management section, which may reveal details such as soils that are too sandy to support wildlife browsing.

A user can export the reports to spreadsheet and word processing software programs. The user also can summarize the Soil Data Explorer information using the Soil Reports tab. These soil reports list each soil type, along with a summary table of the salient characteristics for each category analyzed. For example, the report on Land Classifications can generate an analysis of the soils classified as farmlands. The report identifies which soils are prime farmland and which are not. The Building Site Development report lists the limitations of each soil type for different categories of buildings, along with the sources of limitations. These reports provide a vast amount of information about the land. All of these reports can be added to the Shopping Cart for a custom report of soils of the AOI. Although this step is called a Shopping Cart, there is no charge for the report.

The user then goes to Check Out to produce the final report. WSS generates a Custom Soil Resource Report. At this stage, users can enter a subtitle and choose map options from the Report Properties dialog box to produce a customized pdf file. Users can also preview and edit their custom reports in the Table of Contents panel before check out.

Landowners can combine the information gleaned from the soil survey to estimate production and income potential for their properties. For example, calculating the soil's carrying capacity is the first step in estimating income potential from a grazing lease (see the reference Gilliland, "Ranching for Rookies"). The data will also enable an owner or potential buyer to compare results from current management with expected results.

In addition to providing individual analyses, the WSS can generate reports on soils for entire counties. The Soil Data Explorer allows a comparison of the relative productivity of all soils in the county. The map helps users to identify the most productive soils in the region, thus assisting in the search for areas to explore.

Learning to use the website requires patience because of the massive amount of data it contains. However, those willing to devote the time needed to explore its wealth of information will find the Web Soil Survey invaluable in evaluating land resources.

United States Geological Survey (USGS)

Topographic maps trace changes in elevation. The relief of the landscape emerges as a set of contour lines overlaid on maps that feature details such as roads, streams, buildings, and towns. Each contour line identifies points on the map that lie at specific levels of elevation above sea level. Nearby contour lines trace another level of elevation. For example, one contour labeled "1,500" might have a series of unlabeled contours

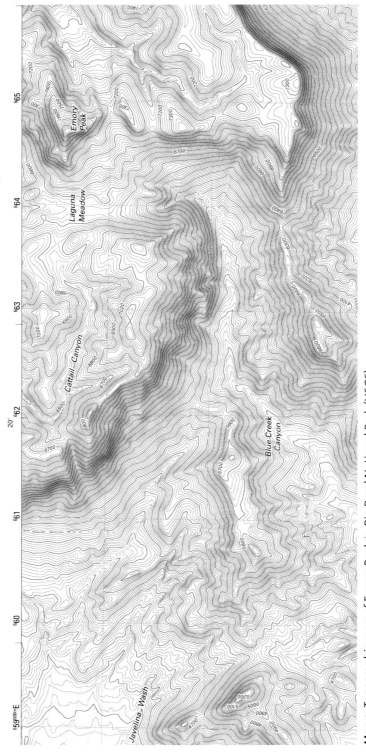

Map 2. Topographic map of Emory Peak in Big Bend National Park (USGS).

U.S. DEPARTMENT OF THE INTERIOR
U. S. GEOLOGICAL SURVEY

The National Map
US Topo

Map 3. Combined photographic and topographic map of Emory Peak in Big Bend National Park (USGS).

Map 4. Aerial photograph of Emory Peak in Big Bend National Park (USGS).

intervening between the fifteen-hundred-foot contour and the next heavy contour, labeled "1,600." Moving from the first labeled contour to the second represents an increase in elevation of one hundred feet. When a map contains ten contour lines between the fifteen-hundred- and sixteen-hundred-foot level, each contour represents an elevation change of ten feet. Examining the relative elevation of the main contours establishes an indication of hills or valleys. Rising numbers on the main contours indicate terrain has sloped upward, and when walking the land you would be climbing a hill. If the numbers on the contours are decreasing, you would be walking down a slope. The accompanying figures are examples of USGS online maps. The first shows a traditional topographic map of Emory Peak in Big Bend National Park, with contour lines at twenty-foot intervals. The second image displays the same contours overlaid on an aerial photographic map. The third image shows the rugged features of this site, without the contours.

The distance between contours indicates the intensity of elevation change. If contours lie far apart, the corresponding terrain will be relatively flat, while an area with contours packed closely together indicates sudden elevation changes associated with mountains and canyons. By examining a topographic map of each candidate property, the buyer can gain a preliminary insight into each landscape. A buyer or owner can access and download USGS maps at http://www.usgs.gov/. Buyers and owners can also find and purchase these USGS maps at many locations throughout the country.

Other Map Resources

Many other government agencies besides the USGS also offer specialized maps and GIS applications. Texas appraisal districts maintain a complete set of ownership maps for all land in their districts. Many districts make these maps available online. In addition to the soil surveys from the NRCS, the USDA offers a wide array of map products from several agencies or services, including the Farm Service Agency (FSA). All of these maps can be accessed through the Geospatial Data Gateway at http://datagateway.nrcs.usda.gov. The General Land Office (GLO) in Texas offers an array of maps at http://www.glo.texas.gov, as does the Texas Commission on Environmental Quality (TCEQ), at http://www.tceq.state.tx.us/comm_exec/forms_pubs/maps/. Many of the maps at these sites are extremely detailed and thus may impose a burden on users who must learn how the systems operate. The systems will, however, reward the persistent user with access to very useful information.

Visual On-Site Inspections

Prospective landowners should walk the entire candidate tract carefully, noting all of its features. By identifying properties with characteristics that threaten to undermine efficient management, buyers can eliminate unsuitable candidates. Studying soil surveys and topographic maps can help a buyer to identify which properties would be unsuitable for their purposes. However, buying a property based simply on study of a map or collection of photos would be an extremely risky venture. An onsite inspection can help a buyer avoid paying for sought-after features that do not actually exist on the property.

An inspection begins with a drive to the property. Armed with a preselected list of features to check, the buyer should begin this phase of the inspection with a keen awareness of the countryside. If the land becomes his or her property, the new owner will experience that trip many times in the years to come. Pay attention to land uses along the way, taking note of the appearance they create. Do they create a pleasant environment, or is there an inharmonious use that threatens to be a nuisance? Is there a noisy highway or railroad tracks nearby that create loud distractions?

Enjoy the trip, but keep an eye out for problems. Nuisance land uses would not only perturb the landowner during his or her tenure but also threaten to diminish the property's appeal should the owner choose to sell in the future. When hot markets fuel competition for available properties, buyers frequently ignore this kind of negative influence. However, a savvy buyer will realize that ignoring negative elements in the local environment adds to the risk of landownership.

The prospective buyer should also investigate plans for changes in the environment. For example, the installation of poultry-raising facilities nearby may impact the property and community. A public utility planning a new transmission line might have targeted the property or a neighboring property for the path of the line. Those plans might kill the deal or they may simply lead to a reduced price to offset the risk of suffering an unsightly intrusion in the countryside.

When visiting the property, make an inventory of existing improvements. Find out which structures will remain after the sale. Do hunting blinds stay? What about wildlife feeders? Who owns the wildlife and does it transfer as well? Native white-tailed deer belong to the State of Texas, but introduced exotics such as fallow deer belong to individuals. If they are present, the seller could either include them in the deal or sell them separately as personal property. Although existing structures may not serve a buyer's plan for the property, they may still have utility. Every barn and shed can contribute to planned activities or be converted to alternative uses. Some structures may present no obvious use but would be costly to remove. Always determine which structures would be included in the purchase.

Keep an eye out for visible household dumps. Mattresses, broken furniture, and discarded tires create an eyesore, but old refrigerators and containers that held pesticides or herbicides may indicate the presence of toxic chemicals or other dangerous conditions.

Identify the complement of utilities available at the site. Verify that electric service extends to the tract. Check out the telephone service, including cellular signals. One new rural land buyer reported to her provider that there was no service on her land. The provider assured her that improvements were on the way, but they were not. A year later, she switched to another provider and finally had acceptable service. Find out about access to water, gas, trash pickup, and high-speed Internet. Notice the condition of access roads and verify who is responsible for maintaining them. This initial visit is the time to discover potential problems.

Buyers should also be on the lookout for evidence of problems with septic systems. Ensure that the system is located far enough away from water wells to avoid contamination. If an obvious flow emanates from a septic tank, the system needs immediate attention. If no obvious flows appear, ask the owner or agent about the system's condition. Flush the toilets and run water in sinks and wash basins to see how fast they drain. Sluggish flows indicate the system has problems. However, just because the system passes tests on the day of inspection does not mean all is well. Buyers should negotiate an allowance for the seller to correct problems within a specific period. The Texas Commission on Environmental Quality (TCEQ) has specified parameters for installation of on-site sewage facilities that installers must follow. Local counties can adopt stricter standards, but the TCEQ specifications apply as minimums. The specifications require a distance of at least fifty feet between septic tanks and wells or cisterns. Check with TCEQ or the county health department to find out about the kinds of systems allowed, specific installation requirements, and recommended maintenance schedules for them. Heavy soils may require use of expensive aerobic systems that need constant maintenance. Observe flaws in and physical wear and tear on buildings that will require repairs. Note the placement and condition of fences and corrals. Obvious shortcomings suggest the need for near-term repair or replacement. Estimating the costs of rehabilitating the physical improvements reduces the chance of facing unanticipated expenses after a purchase.

Ask about mineral extraction on the property. If the mineral rights do not transfer with the land sale, a new owner may experience unpleasant disruptions if mineral owners decide to explore for gas or oil. In legal terms, the mineral estate takes precedence over the surface estate, meaning that the owners of the mineral rights may drill whenever they please. A buyer might reasonably expect future drilling activity in areas where drilling rigs are currently operating.

Observe the presence of any mineral extraction activity in the wider local area as well. The drilling management practices of oil and gas producers vary, with some cutting corners or otherwise creating problems for landowners. Look for unusual stains on the soil and other obvious signs of contamination. Identify old well sites, and inspect them for potentially hazardous conditions, such as pipes or rods protruding from the ground. Evidence of such problems may indicate the need for more rigorous examination to reduce the risk of acquiring a contaminated property.

When the property features stands of growing timber, trellised grapevines, or producing orchards, buyers need specialized expertise to evaluate the physical condition of the timber or other permanent plantings. Observing the aesthetic configuration of the vegetation does little to assess the strength and reliability of the resource. A potential buyer may find it beneficial to identify and engage advisors with expertise in the types of land and crops under consideration.

Property Inspection Checklist

Section 5.008 of the Texas Property Code requires a seller to disclose the condition of residential real property for a single home. The code lists items that must be acknowledged and known defects that must be described. Although the list is comprehensive, it is not intended to take the place of a thorough inspection by the buyer. Buyers of rural properties should note that section 5.008 does not apply to rural properties with more than one dwelling or nonresidential structures. Buyers can use the checklist offered here to guide them in a thorough inspection of candidate properties. The list addresses some important aspects of the property that buyers should consider as they weigh the advantages and disadvantages of each potential tract. Details on some of the items in the list are discussed in later chapters. The inspections should verify not only the presence or absence of the items but also their condition, the responsibility for maintenance, and the expected life. A buyer may deem it prudent to engage experts to evaluate these and similar items.

Infrastructure
- Access: Do roads, bridges, culverts, and rights of way provide convenient access to the property? Are these items in good condition? Who is responsible for maintaining these items?
- Water: Are wells in good condition and supplying sufficient water for planned uses?
- Drainage: Does water flow easily off of the property? Is there underground drainage tile? Are drainage ditches clean and efficient?
- Sewer service
- Electric service
- Telephone service
- Television signal or service
- High-speed Internet services
- Trash disposal
- Mail service
- School bus routes

Improvements
- Houses
- Barns
- Camp houses
- Storage facilities
- Animal pens
- Wells
- Septic systems
- Fences
- Roads

Neighborhood
- Appearance
- Neighboring land uses
- Highways

- Railroads
- Subdivisions
- Nuisances
- Environmental factors
- Contamination
- Endangered animals
- Endangered plants
- Dumps and clutter

What Goes and What Stays
- Buildings
- Fixtures
- Wildlife
- Crops
- Other improvements (hunting blinds, feeders)

Correspondence with Planned Uses
- Soil productivity
- Soil mechanical properties
- Configuration of boundaries
- Elevations and depressions
- Ease of access to and within the property

Physical Condition
- Streets and roads
- Condition of improvements
- Environmental contamination

Surveyed Boundaries
- Fence lines
- Visible easements
- Potential areas of dispute with neighbors

Local Communities
- Local installation and repair services
- Extraterritorial jurisdictional boundaries of towns and cities
- Schools
- Pending projects involving eminent domain proceedings

Evaluating Economic Influences and Trends

6

A tree grows
between paddocks
at Lane's End Farm.
Photograph by
Charles E. Gilliland

Land value arises from the configuration created by the current social setting and the resource endowments found on the land. Together they form the basis of activity that generates returns to landowners. The array of current land prices reflects a summary of individuals' assessments of the value created when the land is dedicated to their envisioned uses. Buyers reveal their personal estimated value through their offers to buy. Presumably, those offers would extend up to the highest valuation of his or her planned use. Those individual assessments presumably also incorporate personal forecasts of value growth anticipated from projected future uses. Essentially, the market serves as a medium communicating an array of prices reflecting individual valuations by both buyers and sellers, given an anticipated economic and social environment.

Before making a land purchase, potential buyers should ask a series of critical questions about current and future social and economic conditions that could affect the buyer's ownership experience, the value of the land, and the ultimate disposal of the property. What type of economic environment is supporting current price levels? Will the local community thrive and expand into the countryside? How will in-migration contribute to future growth? Do area residents earn enough to be able to pay property taxes and keep up with maintenance costs? Will future conditions lead to higher prices or declining values? Each potential buyer must formulate answers to these and other questions as they evaluate prospective sites for purchase.

To avoid the risk of harboring unrealistic expectations, potential buyers should evaluate how current and potential future conditions could affect the set of assumptions they have made about candidate properties. By consulting a wide array of resources, a potential buyer can assess the apparent reliability of their expectations. Although many in the public believe they have a firm grasp of economic developments, checking real facts can help to dispel unrealistic hopes. Examining these influences in their current configurations provides a context for today's economic performance, while examining trends in the past can offer insight into how the parameters might vary in the future. In short, the buyer can gain an appreciation for the contemporary economic context and an appreciation for which economic influences might substantially affect forecast conditions.

National and Local Conditions

Local economic influences supporting various land uses depend on community employment patterns. Those patterns also depend on conditions and prospects for state, regional, and national market activity. Assumptions of a robust economy with rising values ahead may prompt sellers to hold out for unrealistic prices when circumstances point to emerging economic weakness. Buyers foreseeing a soaring economy might impulsively jump at a property, whereas a more muted forecast of future developments would likely result in more circumspect offers. This variation in forecasts affects the mix of properties changing hands. When buyers anticipate robust economic activity and strong demand for land, their emphasis is on finding something, in some cases anything, to buy. Muted expectations free the buyer to concentrate on the quality of each property in a more relaxed market environment. Thus, difficult economic circumstances lead buyers to concentrate on quality. Both buyers and sellers can tap an assemblage of information and projections to assist them in their decision making.

Publications offered by the Federal Reserve Board provide a good beginning. Eight times each year the Fed publishes the Beige Book, which reports current economic conditions as seen through the eyes of bank officials and other business contacts. The report covers the national picture and includes individual summaries for each of the twelve districts in the system. Summaries of the information generally find their way into various news outlets. However, the actual publication contains many details that never reach the popular media.

The full report contains a summary of current activity and trends in seven different sectors of the economy for each of the twelve Federal Reserve districts, as well as an overall summary. The report begins with a detailed description of consumer spending and tourism observed in each district. The analysis continues with narrative descriptions of developments in nonfinancial services, manufacturing, real estate and construction, banking and finance, agriculture and natural resources, employment and wages, and prices. The reports reflect interviews with local experts in each district. The information provides a snapshot of the conventional wisdom in the various areas of the country about local economic conditions. Readers gain an appreciation for the broad variation in conditions around the country. The report may be accessed at http://www.minneapolisfed.org/bb/.

Southwest Regional Conditions

In addition to providing this moving snapshot of the current economy, many Fed member banks compile data and prepare reports on past economic conditions. The Dallas district of the Federal Reserve publishes statistics and reports on the regional economy for the Southwest, including Texas, New Mexico, and Louisiana. By going to the district's website, http://www.dallasfed.org/research/regional.cfm, and clicking on Texas Economic Conditions and Outlook, Construction and Real Estate, Texas Exports, Mexico, Agriculture, or Energy, anyone can access valuable up-to-date economic information.

The Dallas Fed website contains a section, labeled Economic Research, where district staff present the results of their research. These quarterly reports contain vital information about current economic conditions in the three states served by the Dallas Fed. In addition, using the Economic Data section, a potential buyer or seller can gauge the health of the economy by exploring information on trends in important economic indicators. Analyzing the contents should give individuals an indication of the relative strength of economic activity in the region, as well as hints about likely developments in the future. The site includes leading indicators, employment trends, manufacturing activity, and estimates of agricultural land values.

Historical National Conditions

Information on national conditions is available from the Federal Reserve Economic Data (FRED) collection of economic time series on a number of recognized measures of economic activity. See http://www.research.stlouisfed.org/fred2/.

Focus on Texas Conditions

The Real Estate Center in the Mays Business School at Texas A&M University actively maintains a website with a great deal of information about the Texas economy: http://www.recenter.tamu.edu/. The site features monthly economic updates on all aspects of employment and economic activity in Texas. In addition to this statewide information, the center reports on twenty-five metropolitan statistical area markets. The DATA tab on the website contains links to housing data, as well as data on building permits, employment and unemployment, population, and rural land markets. The center is the best resource for quick access to vital and in-depth information for real estate market participants. The entire site and the center's publications are designed to help market participants make sound decisions in their real estate transactions.

Other Resources

Information abounds in the age of the Internet. No listing of such re-sources could hope to include all of the useful repositories. Some espe-cially useful sites that address land market developments, agricultural trends, and crop conditions are as follows:

- LandOwner Newsletter, published at ProFarmer, with reports on land market developments throughout the country, http://www .profarmer.com/Blogs/tabid/64/BlogID/1/Default.aspx
- Agricultural & Food Policy Center, Texas A&M University (AFPC), which reports on issues affecting farmers and ranchers, including projected crop prices and enterprise profitability, http://www.afpc .tamu.edu/
- Doane's Agricultural Services, http://www.doane.com/
- National Agricultural Statistical Service (NASS), part of the USDA, http://www.nass.usda.gov/
- Texas and Southwestern Cattle Raisers Association, http://www .texascattleraisers.org/index.html
- Texas State Data Center, http://www.txsdc.utsa.edu/

Economic Conditions Checklist

Buyers can use the following checklist to guide their analysis of the economic realities of today's land markets and the potential for future changes:

National Economic Conditions
- Gross domestic product (GDP) levels and trends
- Employment
- Incomes

Local Economic Conditions
- Income
- Employment

- Possible developments

Specific Economic Impacts on Potential Uses

- Projected population growth
- Crop prices
- Input prices

Buyers should not anticipate that all data gathered for this checklist from the sources mentioned above will trace out unambiguous trends. National and regional trends often diverge, while patterns in income, population, and employment frequently present confusing portraits of the state of the underlying economy. Dealing with these anomalies can be trying. Even seasoned observers can and often do disagree about the implications of current developments. Substantial rewards often accrue to individuals who interpret trends before they become obvious to all. As underlying economic trends emerge more clearly, their impact on land prices will become easier to discern.

Identifying Legal Rights and Limitations

7

The Harrison County Courthouse in Marshall protects documents and entertains action to protect property owners' rights. Photograph by Diane Gilliland

Buyers can realize their land use dreams only if the assumptions they make about the future are reasonably on target. The validity of those assumptions depends critically on the package of rights that transfer with the purchase. At the most elemental level, property rights in land consist of rights to use the land and to secure the fruits of that use. Typically, buyers assume that their purchase entitles them to pursue land use plans free from outside interference. Buyers fall in love with the streams and hills of their land acquisition, but it is the legal context of ownership that actually determines future use of their land. Legal limitations imposed by governments or resulting from former owners' actions can invalidate plans for use based on faulty assumptions. For example, a buyer planning to develop an equine facility may see plans frustrated by a conservation easement granted by a previous owner. In the process of searching for a property, potential buyers should carefully evaluate all legal influences affecting candidate sites to identify potential impediments to selected uses.

Verifying Ownership

A critical investigative step before purchasing a property is verifying that a prospective seller actually owns the land. One young couple found a perfect spot in the country and approached the nearest house, where they explained to the resident that they would like to buy the acreage and pay cash for it. The resident in the home quickly offered to sell, and the deal was sealed. The "seller" prepared a quitclaim deed and exchanged it for the cash the couple offered. This "seller" had duped the young couple. They thought they had paid for ownership rights to the land, but the seller's document transferred only the rights this neighboring landowner possessed. The deed did not guarantee any degree of ownership. This kind of chicanery represents an extreme that almost never occurs, but buyers do need to check records to be sure the potential seller actually can deliver the property. Otherwise, a buyer can waste valuable time and effort on a property that is not for sale.

Verifying ownership involves knowledge about the system of land ownership in Texas. Searching for evidence of actual ownership involves data that buyers can access in various places, locally or in Austin. Originally, all land in Texas belonged to the government of Spain, then Mexico, the Republic of Texas, and the State of Texas. From the 1500s to the end of the 1800s most of that territory shifted from public ownership to private hands. That transfer required creation of a system to record and verify private land titles. The General Land Office (GLO) of the State of Texas developed the system currently used to administer the land grant process. The GLO first granted qualified candidates a land certificate for a specified amount of land. The amount of acreage granted depended on the candidate meeting specific criteria and agreeing to certain conditions to qualify for the grant. Those criteria and conditions varied over the years. Then the candidate filed field notes (a written account of the land survey) with the GLO. After fulfilling conditions of the grant (such as making improvements and paying fees) the individual could apply for the patent (original title), which the GLO ultimately granted.

A patent is the legal instrument transferring land from the public domain to private ownership. In Texas, the set of records, or title, documenting land grants from the periods of Spanish and Mexican sovereignty provided proof of ownership, and the State of Texas recognized those grants. With a few exceptions, documentation of title to all privately held land in Texas begins with a patent issued by the GLO.

Few landowners ever see the patent, however, because the county clerk's office in each Texas county now administers property transfers. When a property ownership transfer takes place, the buyer files with the county clerk an instrument (usually a warranty deed) to document that transfer. The filing serves as notice to the public that the property has changed hands. Repeated sales of the same property create evidence of a chain of title in the clerk's documents.

County clerks maintain an index of sellers (grantors) and buyers (grantees) for all property transactions. Although offices vary in the level of technology they employ, all counties provide a means to search these records. This access allows an individual to go to the clerk with the current property owner's name and trace the history of title transfers for the property through the names of previous owners found in the deed records.

Appraisal districts are another useful information source because they maintain records on all properties in a county. Although the quality of these records varies, appraisal districts routinely maintain a set of maps identifying the owners of each parcel of taxable real estate. Those maps relate to corresponding appraisal records that should identify all important buildings on each tract of land, along with estimates of their taxable value. Many appraisal districts have posted ownership information on their websites. Although buyers should not rely on the accuracy of these records without verifying the information at the county clerk's office, the appraisal district websites are a good place to start looking for the current owner of record.

For a variety of reasons, owners may have failed to undertake the proper steps to patent some privately held land. This situation frequently arises from inaccurate original surveys. For example, if the field notes missed a small parcel in the legal description of the original survey, that parcel was not included in the field notes filed to obtain the patent. Unpatented private land is known as a "vacancy." Some owners may not be aware of these title defects, whereas others may know about the vacancies in their landholdings but choose to avoid the expense involved in obtaining a patent from the GLO. Owners with unpatented land face a lengthy process to correct the title. The details of this process are far too intricate to describe here. However, owners of lands with vacancies know that a good-faith claimant has a preferential right to purchase or lease the vacancy from the GLO.

A good-faith claimant must have occupied or used the land for at least ten years. A buyer who acquires land that a seller has occupied or used for ten years or more, believing that he or she owned the land, also qualifies as a good-faith claimant. In some cases, an owner of adjoining land will also qualify as a good-faith claimant. The GLO determines which parties qualify as good-faith claimants.

Before the GLO grants or amends a patent, the claimant must obtain a re-survey of the land and submit the surveyor's report. The required report normally includes field notes, sketches, deeds, abstracts, other surveyors' reports, the surveyor's professional opinion of the original survey's construction, notes on bearings, distances, and landmarks, and professional conclusions based on factual observations. The re-survey process is likely to be expensive.

The particular language in a deed does not necessarily indicate the existence of a valid patent. The only way to verify a property's patent is to trace the chain of title back to the original grant on file with the GLO. With the abstract number for the property and the name of the county in which the property is located, the GLO should be able to verify that a patent was issued. Generally, vacancies are not a problem for most buyers and sellers. However, finding an undisclosed one could cause problems for a landowner. To avoid unpleasant surprises, a buyer should ask the seller if vacancies might exist on the property. However, when a seller knows the property contains unpatented land, the buyer should take note of the possible expense and take the necessary steps to perfect the title to the land.

Identifying Rights Owned

The idea that property consists of a bundle of rights implies that an owner can transfer parts of the bundle while retaining some rights. The absence of specific rights in the bundle to be transferred has impeded or killed many potential transactions. For example, a tract of land subject to a long-term lease restricts an owner's plans for using the land. Acquiring land subject to the lease can effectively create two owners. The tenant owns the usage rights specified in the lease. The buyer retains any other usage options that do not diminish the tenant's right plus a return of those alienated rights when the lease expires. A buyer should investigate any lease arrangements applying to candidate properties to ascertain the extent of control ceded to the tenant, as well as the conditions that result in termination of the tenant's rights. An existing lease need not derail the transaction, but the buyer should negotiate with full knowledge of the impact of any lease agreement on land use plans. The process may include a separate negotiation with the tenant to establish an understanding, or the buyer may acquire the leasehold as well as the leased fee.

Some leases contain a provision granting the tenant a right of first refusal, meaning that the owner must offer to sell the property to the tenant before offering it to anyone else. That clause can cause potential buyers to avoid even making an offer. The time and expense required to develop a reasonable offer impose a considerable burden on would-be buyers. If a tenant can use the potential buyer's carefully devised offer to set his or her own offering price, that prospective buyer has wasted resources to no good end.

Mineral leases transfer control of the land to the operator holding the right to drill. Because the mineral estate is preeminent, other interests' rights are secondary, meaning that the operator can enter the land, drill for oil and gas, and produce product at any time. Each lease agreement specifies conditions for production, but surface owners normally have little to say about well placement and other facets of the drilling operation. Because oil and gas operations can substantially impact land use, potential buyers should clearly identify mineral ownership and the status of existing mineral leases.

Easements grant a third party the right to specified uses of an owner's property, such as crossing another landowner's property to access one's own land. Land subject to an easement has effectively had the bundle of rights narrowed. Because easements imply weakened control by the property owner, buyers should review existing easements on candidate properties. They can represent small concessions by property owners or they may prohibit a wide range of activities, as in the case of conservation easements, which can effectively bar all development.

Sometimes physical indicators hint that an easement exists. For example, a petroleum pipeline easement tracing a cleared lane through a stand of cedar signals its presence to even casual observers. Electrical transmission line easements also are obvious. In contrast, a little used easement allowing access to a neighboring tract may present little visible evidence. Further, a flowage easement allowing neighboring landowners to release floodwaters across a tract only appears obvious when flooding occurs. The buyer needs to inquire about easements early in the process.

Buyers should also inquire about possible environmental contamination. If a past owner dumped toxic substances on the site, the new buyer will inherit liability for any cleanup costs. Look for contamination and ask about it. The cautious buyer might request a professional environmental inspection.

Endangered Species

The presence of habitat for endangered species can substantially impact uses of land. The US Fish and Wildlife Service (FWS) of the Department of the Interior and the National Marine Fisheries Service (NMFS) administer the Endangered Species Act (ESA) for both land- and marine-based species. According to the FWS, Texas may provide habitat for as many as eighty-two endangered and sixteen threatened species. These species range from the blue whale, two of which were reported to have beached on the coast at different times, to the coffin cave mold beetle in Central Texas.

Endangered or threatened status provides species a broad range of protections that can severely restrict how landowners may use their property. To comply with the ESA and maximize property potential, landowners must understand what the act does and does not allow.

Taking an endangered species violates the law, according to section 9(a) (1) (B) of the ESA. Most people interpret the word *taking* in this context to mean capturing or killing an endangered plant or animal. However, the ESA defines the verb *to take* as "to harass, harm, pursue, hunt, shoot, wound, kill, trap, capture, or collect or to attempt to engage in any such conduct." Through regulation, the FWS further defines harm to include any activity that "actually kills or injures wildlife" and incorporates actions "significantly impairing essential wildlife behavioral patterns, including breeding, feeding, or sheltering." Landowners running afoul of the "take" provision face both civil and criminal penalties, with fines ranging from twenty-five thousand to fifty thousand dollars per violation. Penalties could also include up to one year in prison. The language of the ESA states that each action that takes an individual from an endangered species could result in imposition of a penalty. A single incident that involves the "harassing" of several members of an endangered species could thus result in several separate charges, with each violation requiring a separate penalty.

The broad scope of the ESA and the substantial penalties for breaching it make the presence of endangered species or their habitats a critical consideration for both current and prospective landowners. Land market participants would undoubtedly prefer to use a standardized checklist to determine if a given property contains critical habitat and thus evaluate the potential for restrictions on use of a property. However, each endangered species has unique habitat requirements, making it necessary to judge the potential for land use restrictions on a case-by-case basis. To assess the likelihood of future complications, landowners and land buyers should investigate the ecosystem surrounding a property to identify the possible presence of endangered or threatened species. It may be prudent to involve a specialist in endangered species at this step.

Planned activities, such as land development, that would result in the taking of a species generally require a permit from either the FWS or the NMFS. The FWS and NMFS can assist in determining which, if any, proposed actions are likely to result in a take. If land lies in an area with no listed species, ESA restrictions do not apply. If listed species inhabit the region, however, landowners may well discover protected habitat on their land. Land with extensive habitat may see virtually all uses other than providing habitat for the endangered species placed off limits. However, the ESA has evolved to allow some exceptions to the section 9 take prohibition. These options vary depending on the species' status within the listing process and generally may induce an owner to obtain an incidental take permit before initiating the planned activity.

Endangered Species Checklist

To evaluate the potential for encountering endangered species on particular properties, potential buyers should first find out which endangered species may inhabit the area. Next, they should seek information about what types of habitat to look for. This step may require engaging professional assistance to evaluate the situation on the property.

To determine if an endangered or threatened species might inhabit a specific area, potential buyers can begin by searching online for data compiled by government entities:

- County-level listings of endangered species as compiled by the federal FWS, http://www.fws.gov/endangered/
- Endangered species list for each county in Texas, provided by the Texas Parks and Wildlife Department (TPWD), http://www.tpwd .state.tx.us/landwater/land/maps/gis/ris/endangered_species/

Other resources offer information on what specific indicators of endangered species habitat buyers should look for:

- TPWD individual species listings and habitat descriptions, as well as ESA provisions relating to them, at http://www.tpwd.state.tx.us/ huntwild/wild/species/endang/regulations/us/index.phtml
- *Endangered and Threatened Animals of Texas,* by Linda Campbell (1995), which provides detailed descriptions of endangered species and their habitats in Texas, available as a free download at http://www .tpwd.state.tx.us/huntwild/wild/species/endang/index.phtml

Water
and Oil on
the Land

8

Mineral production occurs across the length and breadth
of Texas. Photograph by Robert Beals II

R ights to use and control water can significantly affect property values. To avoid the risk of buying a property with limited water use rights, buyers should take time to become familiar with Texas water laws that apply in their targeted regions.

Buyers investigating water rights must understand the terms used to describe water resources. For example, surface water is water that has reached a defined water course. Water under an owner's land is groundwater. Water rights normally relate to large quantities of water, and allowed usage is measured in acre-feet rather than gallons. An acre-foot is enough water to cover an acre to a depth of one foot. That volume of water equals 325,853.38 gallons and would flood an average football field to a depth of nearly one foot. One of the primary sources of information on water issues is the Texas Water Development Board (TWDB) in Austin (http://www.twdb.state.tx.us/). The TWDB also administers the water planning process for the State of Texas.

Surface Water

Surface water belongs to the State of Texas, and consequently, landowners generally need permission to use water from rivers and streams. Through procedures administered by the Texas Commission on Environmental Quality (TCEQ) landowners can secure the right to use specified amounts of surface water, provided that the watercourse still contains a volume of nonappropriated water. The rights secured by the landowner can be permanent or for limited terms.

The TCEQ and its predecessors have for the most part fully appropriated the surface water in Texas streams. Most of these perpetually appropriated rights set a priority based on the date when the commission or predecessor entities issued a certificate of adjudication or permit. The documents specify the volume of water an owner may divert from the stream each year. The priority established by the state determines access to water when stream flows fall below the amount appropriated. The lowest priority owners are the first to lose the right to divert water, then the next lowest priority entity, and so on as stream flows continue to fall. This hierarchy means that an owner without an approved water right from TCEQ generally cannot pump water for irrigation from a river running through his or her land. A potential buyer should find out if the landowner has the right to divert a specified amount of surface water. Because the rights have value, sellers not listing rights to surface water likely do not own any.

Surface water used for domestic purposes, livestock, or wildlife management is exempt from the permitting process. This exemption means that an owner can divert surface water to use for household purposes or to water livestock. Owners also can build stock tanks to capture surface water. However, the volume of water impounded must not exceed an average of two hundred acre-feet during a year. The two-hundred-acre-foot limit means that an owner may have a little more than sixty-five million gallons on hand. This impoundment exemption also applies when the water is needed for wildlife management. Although other, very limited exemptions exist, almost any envisioned uses of surface water will likely require permission from the TCEQ.

In some areas of Texas, mostly in the southern portion of the state, a water master under TCEQ supervision controls landowner diversions. The water master endeavors to ensure that owners divert only the amount of water allowed by their permit or certificate and no more. In dry years, the limit might be less than the amount specified in the surface water rights documentation. In other words, the right to one hundred acre-feet of water might entitle a landowner to divert only sixty acre-feet in a drought-plagued year. The water master maintains records of owners' water rights and the amounts of water the owners have diverted. Landowners in those areas controlled by a water master must pay for that service.

The involvement of a water master in documenting surface water use dates to a lawsuit filed in the Lower Rio Grande Valley in the early 1950s. The case resulted in a court-directed adjudication of water rights and the requirement that a water master would control water use. The system requires each irrigator to obtain a pumping permit before diverting a specified amount of water at a particular time. Failure to comply is a violation of state law. The water master's office verifies compliance, and the system enforces water rights very effectively.

In other parts of the state, a so-called "honor system" is in effect. Enforcement of surface water usage restrictions is much less effective in those areas because suspected violations must be pursued through complaints filed with the TCEQ in Austin. Describing a similar situation in the Lower Rio Grande Valley prior to the court-ordered use of a water master, one irrigation district manager declared, "All of the users met and reached a 'gentlemen's agreement' that we would share equally in the sacrifice when water supplies ran short during a drought. But when a drought arrived there were no gentlemen to be found. The guys at the north end of the River pumped it dry."

Landowners with surface water rights avoid paying to support a water master's office, but they pay the expense of weakened enforcement. A buyer should determine which enforcement system applies to their candidate properties and how effective that system is in preserving the right to use water in times of drought.

Groundwater

Groundwater rights differ from surface water rights, and most Texas landowners hold a right to water beneath their land. However, there are exceptions to this general rule, and restrictions apply in many areas of the state. Responding to a crisis prompted by a lawsuit filed in federal court under terms of the Endangered Species Act, Texas created the Edwards Aquifer Authority (EAA) to administer withdrawals from the Edwards Aquifer, the underground source of water for San Antonio. The EAA strictly controls groundwater withdrawals within its boundaries as specified by the state. EAA regulations prevent some owners from pumping groundwater in volumes that exceed the amount allowed for domestic use.

When the EAA began operating, landowners who had not previously irrigated saw their supposed right to water under their land vanish. Furthermore, some owners who did obtain from the EAA an adjudicated right to pump groundwater have sold that right to others. Consequently, those landowners also no longer have a right to groundwater.

Until recent years, in areas outside the territory under the control of the EAA, most Texas landowners enjoyed an unlimited right to pump groundwater. That tradition depended on the legal doctrine known as the "rule of capture," which lies at the root of a fundamental disagreement about water rights in Texas. Many landowners believe they own the water beneath their acreage. Others insist that this rule more accurately means that landowners own the water only after they pump it to the surface from a legal well. Litigation headed to the Texas Supreme Court will result in a final ruling on that issue.

To promote management of aquifers in Texas, the legislature significantly strengthened the powers of groundwater conservation districts (GCDs) in 2001. As political entities similar in authority to independent school districts, GCDs preside over a territory described at its creation. The district must strive to protect property owners' rights while preserving groundwater resources. The Texas Water Code instructs groundwater conservation districts to formulate management plans that

- Provide for the most efficient use of groundwater
- Control and prevent waste of groundwater
- Control and prevent subsidence
- Address conjunctive surface water issues
- Address natural resource issues
- Address drought conditions
- Address conservation

To achieve this ambitious set of goals, groundwater conservation districts must adopt rules ensuring that water usage conforms to regional water plans. A district must base its own plans on estimates of available groundwater previously accepted by the Texas Water Development Board. The district rules should use those estimates to establish the total amount of water available and then to allocate it to landowners within their boundaries. However, measures that effectively manage one aquifer may not work as well in another. Consequently, each district searches for an ideal array of regulations applying to landowners subject to the authority of the GCD. In some cases, this arrangement has resulted in neighboring districts above the same aquifer having very different rules. In one area, the GCD might allow landowners to withdraw one acre-foot per acre per year. Across the county line, a neighboring GCD might limit withdrawals to one-fourth of that amount. Such wide variations in water restrictions can materially affect management options for landowners.

Language in the water code specifies that "nothing in this Code shall be construed as depriving or divesting the owners . . . of the ownership or rights, except as those rights may be limited or altered by rules promulgated by a district" (Texas Water Code, chapter 36.002, Ownership of Groundwater). However, subjecting owners to the rules of the groundwater conservation district clearly signals the intent to allow restrictions on an owner's use of groundwater that did not exist under the rule of capture.

GCD rules that have the most impact on landowners are those specifying procedures for registering and permitting wells. In general, owners must register all wells with the district, even the exempted domestic use wells. On tracts larger than ten acres domestic wells that produce twenty-five thousand or fewer gallons per day are exempt from the permitting process, as are wells permitted by the Texas Railroad Commission to oil and gas producers for completion of a permitted oil or gas well. Mineral producers are governed by the Railroad Commission, which issues permits to use as much water as is needed to complete the well. A district may also exempt other wells as the board of directors sees fit; as a result, some GCDs have set limits that allow landowners to pump more than twenty-five thousand gallons per day from exempt wells. However, exempt wells must conform to GCD specifications for casing, pipe, and fittings.

Most wells capable of producing more than twenty-five thousand gallons per day require a permit. The permit may specify the exact location and purpose of the well. It may also require "beneficial use" while imposing certain conditions and limitations on withdrawals. "Beneficial use" is a legal doctrine incorporated into water laws in most states. It requires a water user to make a beneficial use of the water and prohibits waste or nonuse. It has been described as a "very elastic" concept that is often defined by a court of law after a suit has been tried. Permit requirements normally apply to drilling and completing new wells or altering the size of existing wells.

The Texas Water Code allows GCDs to consider how granting a new permit will affect existing permit holders and surface water resources. This provision allows for the possibility of enacting rules that protect historical users to the detriment of new applicants. While the code requires "fair and impartial" district rules, it specifies that districts may "preserve historic use before the effective date of the rules to the maximum extent practicable." Thus, the GCD can adopt more stringent rules for new permit applications than those applied to existing permit holders. Any new restrictions must apply to all new users, as well as to owners increasing output from existing wells. The code does not identify the extent of protection historical users may receive, but historical users and new users clearly may face vastly different requirements to obtain a permit. Districts can adopt different rules for different aquifers, subdivisions of aquifers, or geologic strata.

Rule differences should not be arbitrary and must bear some reasonable relationship to the management plan of the GCD. Although district boards cannot prohibit water exports, they may regulate them and charge export fees. Local approaches adopted by GCDs to manage groundwater vary greatly across Texas. Many districts may face litigation as they enact rules curtailing unregulated withdrawal and transfer of groundwater.

Prospective buyers should investigate the current rules of any district governing water withdrawals on candidate properties before negotiating a deal.

Spurred by a state water planning initiative that began in 1997, municipalities have also begun to secure water rights to support future growth. As an ongoing effort, the search for supplies of water has created the potential for landowners to sell water rights or lease water to these municipal users. Most activity has focused on groundwater. Mindful of potential windfalls, some sellers of land have reserved commercial rights to the groundwater under the land they are selling, essentially stripping that right from the bundle of property rights being transferred and leaving only the rights to groundwater for domestic use and watering livestock. Buyers should verify whether or not commercial water rights currently remain with the land and if they will transfer when the property sells.

Development Water Supplies

Special circumstances apply to buyers planning to develop land. In some cases, suppliers of utilities may have obtained the exclusive right to provide water and/or wastewater service for all land located in a particular area. The TCEQ issues "certificates of convenience and necessity" (CCNs) to applicants offering to provide specified utility services to a particular geographic area. Technically, the CCN obligates the holder to provide the specified service to anyone in the area requesting service. The supplier must provide continuous, adequate service. Once a supplier obtains a CCN, no one else can provide the covered service.

Some developers who have acquired land for housing subdivisions and planned to install and operate a water system to supply the new homeowners discover that a local utility held a CCN covering their land. Developers in this situation would have to negotiate with the CCN holder or undertake a bureaucratic process to extricate the subdivision from coverage by the CCN. Buyers envisioning the possibility of development should investigate to determine if any CCNs apply to candidate properties.

Buyers should check with local water supply utilities and the TCEQ to identify CCNs covering the subject properties. Local offices of water supply corporations, water supply districts, municipalities, and other special districts should know which areas lie within the coverage areas for CCNs that they hold. In addition, the TCEQ maintains an online mapping system called the Water Utilities Map Viewer that shows the boundaries of existing CCN areas; see http://www.tceq.state.tx.us/gis/iwudview.html. If one or more CCNs apply to the property and development might occur sometime in the future, the buyer should investigate the policies and procedures used by the CCN holders to foresee possible complications in future development plans.

The formal process for planning future water usage that the State of Texas instituted in 1997 relies on Regional Water Planning Groups to develop studies of anticipated needs and supplies. The process is designed to proactively plan water projects for a growing population. The Texas Water Development Board works with the Regional Water Planning Groups to develop a statewide water plan. The 2007 version of that plan, as well as each of the sixteen regional water plans, is available at the TWDB website, http://www.twdb.state.tx.us/.

As noted earlier, local groundwater conservation districts also control groundwater use in many areas of Texas. To identify rules and regulations governing the use of groundwater, a buyer should read the GCD rules prior to a making a land purchase. District rules vary substantially from place to place.

Water Availability Checklist

Access to water can make or break property owner plans for specific uses. Furthermore, not having water rights may impede prospects for selling the land when an owner is ready to exit. Buyers should investigate the status of rights for both surface water and groundwater.

Surface Water
- Identify whether or not surface water rights transfer with the land
- Find out if a water master controls stream diversions

Groundwater
- Determine if the land lies within the Edwards Aquifer Authority
- Identify any groundwater conservation district with jurisdiction over the land
- Identify any certificates of convenience and necessity applying to the land
- Investigate the reliability of water supplies
- Investigate the quantity of groundwater available

- Investigate the quality of the water supplies
- Obtain estimates of pumping and/or diversion costs

The Texas Commission on Environmental Quality maintains a list of resources that will assist individuals in researching water laws and regulations. These resources, including maps of GCDs, are at http://www .tceq.state.tx.us/permitting/water_supply/groundwater/districts.html. The Texas Alliance of Groundwater Conservation Districts maintains links to member district websites at http://www.texasgroundwater.org/ Links.html. Buyers can access most districts' information from that site, where they will also find a listing of GCD rules.

Oil and Gas

With the exception of so-called mineral classified land, for which the state retains all mineral rights, Texas landowners hold title to oil and gas beneath the surface of their acreage unless a previous owner reserved those rights or a mineral lease exists for the land. Long ago, the Texas Supreme Court ruled that the mineral estate is dominant over the surface estate when questions of access arise. That means that the mineral estate owner can occupy "as much of the surface as is reasonably necessary" to explore for and develop oil and gas deposits.

Much litigation has addressed the issue of "reasonably necessary" in this legal specification. Some of the practices validated by Texas courts include

- Conducting geophysical explorations on the surface
- Selecting the best potential well sites
- Constructing, maintaining, and using roads, bridges, canals, and other passageways necessary to transport materials, personnel, and equipment to and from the well sites
- Using caliche found on leased premises
- Housing employees

This abbreviated list indicates the potential for many activities that could interfere with surface owners' quiet enjoyment of their land. Furthermore, Texas courts have found that mineral leases actually transfer ownership rights to the lessee. That means the lessee's rights also supersede those of the surface owner. Therefore, a mineral reservation or mineral lease creates conditions that could threaten surface owners' planned activities. In addition, the mineral extraction process may alter the appearance of the landscape.

To avoid unpleasant surprises, buyers should verify the state of mineral ownership on candidate properties. Because of the threat of disruption to enjoyment of their property, prospective land buyers have increasingly tended to avoid properties with existing oil and gas leases. In addition, buyers increasingly tend to shun properties where reservations of rights in the past have split the mineral estate from the surface estate. When prospective buyers want land for recreational purposes, it makes little sense to buy a property where unsightly industrial equipment would interfere with recreation and make a future sale difficult.

The risks associated with potential oil and gas production need not summarily disqualify candidate properties from consideration. However, potential buyers striving to maintain maximum control of the land should thoroughly investigate the status of the mineral estate.

Gathering and analyzing information can help potential buyers mitigate risks created by separation of the mineral estate from the surface estate. The investigation should strive to establish the state of mineral ownership in a series of steps. First, directly observe the condition of currently producing wells and associated facilities. Poorly maintained sites with unsightly tanks and pump jacks may summarily disqualify a candidate property. Even well-maintained installations may give pause to potential buyers. If the buyer can anticipate that wells currently in place will likely continue production, the investigation should include inquiries about the management practices of operators. The analysis should also verify the language of leases and division orders. These documents control activity allowed on the surface of the land. Potential buyers should have these documents evaluated by an attorney who practices oil and gas production law. Only by intensively examining the documents can buyers hope to understand how oil and gas production will affect their land management plans on specific properties. This time-consuming and potentially expensive hurdle has prompted many to simply avoid land where mineral rights do not transfer to the buyer.

Oil and Gas Production Checklist

• Is there existing or anticipated oil and gas production in the area?
• Is there oil or gas production on the candidate property?

- Who owns the mineral estate?
- Will the mineral rights transfer to the buyer?
- What proportion of the minerals will transfer?
- Is there an existing lease of mineral interests on the land?
- What are the terms of any mineral leases?
- Will absence of minerals affect collateral value of the land?

In addition to these factors that weaken landowner control, buyers should be aware of other possible reservations of rights or leases. For example, lignite and uranium deposits are not considered minerals under the law, so reservations of mineral rights generally only apply to oil and gas in Texas. However, these other potentially valuable substances might also represent sources of risk to would-be buyers. In addition to outright reservations, some land owners have executed long-term leases for these resources. Some lignite leases run for forty years or more. Reservations of wind rights have also begun to surface in land sales. A buyer should verify that reservations of rights do not apply to candidate properties. If such encumbrances do exist, the controlling documents deserve close scrutiny so that the prospective buyer can ascertain the limits they impose on an owner's control over the land. They need not scuttle the deal, but a buyer should avoid the shock of discovering a potential problem after the fact.

To ensure that they are taking the right risk, potential buyers should investigate these and all factors that might have a negative impact on quiet enjoyment of the property. The purpose of the checklists is not to disqualify properties so much as to alert buyers that potential risks may lurk in the deal. This search exercise should help eliminate unpleasant surprises in the future.

Closing the
Deal and Enhancing
Returns

9

A profusion of paintbrush colors the Washington County countryside
near Independence. Photograph by Robert Beals II

Having explored the market and identified a prospective farm or ranch to purchase, the potential buyer must shift from the search mode to securing ownership. Most transactions involve a complement of professionals assisting in the process. The Texas Real Estate Commission has created a farm and ranch transfer of ownership contract that addresses many pre-identified sources of risk and offers several steps to take that should defuse potential threats.

This nine-page document came about after a committee of lawyers and brokers collaborated in identifying common problems in sales of rural land. Such problems generally arose when participants neglected to resolve issues before passing title to the new owner. Although the form was not designed for use without the assistance of properly licensed professionals, a buyer may find it enlightening to examine the twenty-four separate items the document addresses. At the very least, a review of the form provides insights into how the process will unfold. The Texas Real Estate Commission offers the contract form, as well as a list of additional items that may be needed to secure the deal, at its website, http://www .trec.state.tx.us/formslawscontracts/forms/forms-contracts.asp.

The long menu of addenda that follows an introductory notice on the website hints at the possible complexity of the deal. The Farm and Ranch Contract form addresses twenty-four separate issues that could potentially lead to misunderstandings or mistakes in the process of transferring ownership. The items vary from mundane recitation of names of buyers and sellers to specification of closing cost responsibilities.

Buyers should insist on timely delivery of all promised documents at the beginning of the acquisition process. To minimize risk, the buyer should engage the services of professionals early in the process. If the buyer located the property without using an experienced real estate broker who specializes in rural properties, consulting with such a professional can provide guidance during the process of transferring ownership. Buyers should also engage an attorney to review documents and advise them during the acquisition process. For example, an attorney may advise tying deadlines to events in the process rather than specifying dates. This tactic may help potential buyers to secure a refund of earnest money should problems arise. In addition, the practiced eye of an attorney is essential when mineral rights issues are involved.

To ensure accurate property boundaries, insist on an updated survey. When substantial time has passed since the previous survey, fence lines may have strayed from the legally specified boundaries. A new survey allows the buyer to deal with boundary issues before actually acquiring the land. Surveyed metes and bounds as well as the location of easements can be especially critical when years or decades have passed since the last survey.

Buyers should take steps to protect their acquisition by considering a title insurance policy. When the transaction involves a mortgage loan, the lender will likely require such a policy to protect its interest. Because of the risk of a substantial loss, buyers should also consider acquiring a title insurance policy. Should title defects arise after a purchase, title insurance restores losses resulting from deficiencies in ownership rights, including unpaid property taxes, irrigation charges, or competing ownership claims.

It is worth repeating that enlisting these professionals provides buyers with strong protection against taking the wrong risk.

After dealing with potential sources of risk in the acquisition process, landowners assume ownership of an asset capable of conferring a set of anticipated benefits. However, owners also assume a set of responsibilities. As new owners embark on projects to manage their land, they face an array of costs associated with landownership. Foremost among the liabilities is the obligation to pay property taxes. In addition, undertaking specific improvements to the land frequently involves sizable costs that can add up quickly. The new owner should seek out all measures that promise to reduce or limit property ownership costs.

New owners may wish to implement strategies designed to limit property-related expenses or to enhance revenues received from the land. Various programs and legally prescribed revenue enhancements can increase returns from landownership.

Such programs generally target lands dedicated to particular uses and offer subsidies designed to encourage owners to continue or expand those uses. The incentives normally either reduce the taxes owed or provide direct payments to owners who participate. Tax incentives can come from state or local governments or may even come in the form of deductions from federal income tax. Cost-sharing programs and lease payments may provide direct cash income. New owners should search for programs or benefits that encourage adoption of management plans that mesh well with their envisioned use of the land. Each program typically specifies a set of criteria that the property must have or that the owners must meet in order to receive the benefits.

Property Tax Measures

Owners of rural land in Texas can limit their tax liability by taking advantage of special options available to qualified land, as specified in the Texas Property Tax Code. Landowners can potentially qualify for taxation under the agricultural use or open-space taxation provisions. Homestead exemptions also reduce tax burdens for owners occupying a home on the land as their primary residence. However, none of these provisions apply automatically, and each requires an owner to make a special application.

When land values began to escalate in the 1960s, the potential tax burden, driven higher by rapidly rising values, threatened to exceed the entire current income produced on Texas lands used in farming and ranching. The entire return to landowners consisted of that annual agricultural income plus a capital gain realized only when the land was eventually sold. The major portion of total returns came from that capital gain. However, funds from that gain lay far in the future, and the cash from the future capital gain was not available to pay the current tax bill. This mismatch between tax liability and cash resources threatened to tax owners off of their land.

Texans devised a method of taxation that provided for reduced taxes during ownership plus a recapture of a portion of those reduced revenues when an eventual transfer provided the means to pay added taxes. Article VIII, section 1-d, of the Texas Constitution, "Assessment of Lands Designated for Agricultural Use," creates special tax provisions. Land taxed under this provision is sometimes referred to as "1-d land" to differentiate it from land designated in the section "Taxation of Certain Open-Space Land," as established by section 1-d-1 of Article VIII.

Section 1-d was intended to protect bona fide farmers and ranchers from tax levies that surpassed the earning capacity of properties used for agriculture. It requires both the owner and the land to qualify for the preferential treatment established under the 1-d rules. However, under 1-d-1, all owners qualify, and thus only the land must meet certain specified conditions for the owner to obtain the preferred tax treatment.

When land qualifies for 1-d or 1-d-1 taxation, the tax value focuses on net income to the land used in agricultural production. Those so-called agricultural use values normally fall well short of current market value, which is the normal basis for taxing property in Texas. For example, grazing and hunting income on land in the Hill Country may produce a use value of about $70 per acre on land that sells for $5,000 per acre or more. A qualifying owner of qualified land thus pays taxes based on the $70 value. For a tax rate of $2.75 per hundred dollars of taxable value, the market value tax amounts to $137.50 per acre, whereas the 1-d or 1-d-1 tax on the $70 agricultural value would be only $1.93 per acre. Clearly, qualifying for the 1-d or 1-d-1 tax treatment substantially reduces ownership cost.

To capture revenues forgone due to value reduction when the property changes hands or migrates to a nonqualifying use, 1-d taxation imposes an additional tax equal to the difference between taxes based on agricultural use value and those for market value for the previous three years plus interest. For the hypothetical Hill Country assessment, that would amount to an added $135.57 per acre times three, or $412.50 in additional taxes plus interest.

Since the 1-d provision is intended to provide relief from high property taxes for bona fide agricultural producers, agriculture must be the primary occupation and source of income for a qualifying owner. In addition, the land must have been developed or used for agricultural production for the three years immediately preceding the assessment date. Because of the owner qualification requirement, owners must file an application for 1-d treatment each year between January 1 and April 30. Because the 1-d provisions include a very restrictive income source test, few owners apply for the 1-d agricultural use status.

Since most landowners probably cannot list agriculture as their primary occupation and thus cannot qualify for the 1-d tax status, the majority instead choose open-space taxation under section 1-d-1. Because 1-d-1 taxable value is still based on agricultural productivity, it provides some reduction in tax burden. However, 1-d-1 taxation differs from 1-d taxation in several important ways. First, the objective of the legislation creating 1-d-1 taxation concentrated on the environmental goal of preserving open land in the Texas countryside. Nonfarmers and nonranchers faced financial hardship while maintaining rural land in an agricultural use as development washed over the landscape and soaring tax liabilities pressured landowners to sell to developers.

Proponents of 1-d-1 argued that easing the tax bite resulting from market-value based taxation would allow current nonfarm owners to maintain acreage in open-space status and limit urban sprawl. Therefore, section 1-d-1 imposes no income criteria on owners applying for open-space treatment. Only the land must qualify: it must be principally used for either agriculture, to the degree of intensity generally accepted in the area, for five of the preceding seven years or as an ecological laboratory maintained by a public or private college or university.

Land devoted to wildlife management also can qualify for open-space tax treatment. When land use qualifies for wildlife management status under the Property Tax Code, section 23.51, an owner can obtain the agricultural use value without farming the land or grazing livestock. However, owners must actively manage the land to support a thriving population of indigenous animals. The chief appraiser will require an owner to file a well-specified wildlife management plan and follow the steps listed in the plan. The Texas Parks and Wildlife Department provides information on evaluating land and devising wildlife management plans so that a landowner may qualify for this favorable tax treatment (see http://www.tpwd.state.tx.us/landwater/land/private/agricultural_land/). In addition, agents with the AgriLife Extension Service can provide assistance with wildlife management planning. Because of the substantial benefit gained through wildlife management, landowners must properly prepare to apply for the 1-d-1 tax treatment and continue to pursue the practices specified in their management plans. Landowners hoping to qualify for 1-d-1 status under wildlife management provisions can find extensive guidance in "Wildlife Management and Property Tax Valuation in Texas," by Larry Redmon and James Cathey.

The 1-d-1 tax status includes separate provisions for land managed for timber production. Because 1-d-1 status does not require the owner to disclose sources of income to qualify, an owner needs to apply for this status only once, unless the chief appraiser requests another application later.

The annual tax benefit for those with 1-d-1 status generally mirrors that of the 1-d provision. However, a second difference from the 1-d provision results from the measure for imposing the additional tax levied following a change of use. This rollback, as it is called, applies to the difference between taxes based on agricultural use value and those based on market value for up to five years, plus interest of 7 percent annually from the assessment date for each year. Unlike 1-d property transfers, sales of 1-d-1 property do not trigger the rollback tax. Clearly, an owner should consider applying and qualifying for one of these two tax limitation provisions.

The property tax homestead exemption is another measure that reduces ownership costs for landowners with a home on their property. Land under a home does not qualify for agriculture use or open-space tax treatment. However, the house and land may qualify for an array of homestead exemptions, provided that the owners have not claimed those exemptions on a home located elsewhere in Texas. Owners can qualify for the exemptions if they intend to occupy the home as their primary residence. The exemption amounts vary from one jurisdiction to another, and an owner may qualify for several of these exemptions. In addition, school districts and some other tax jurisdictions freeze the annual total tax liability to the amount owed when an owner reaches sixty-five years of age. These homestead provisions can lower ownership costs substantially. An owner must file an application for residence homestead exemptions with the appraisal district where the land is located.

Landowners can find a wealth of information about property tax issues at the website of the Texas Comptroller for Public Accounts, with property tax assistance at

http://www.cpa.state.tx.us/taxinfo/proptax/ and appraisal district sites listed at http://www.cpa.state.tx.us/taxinfo/proptax/apprdir10/.

Conservation Easements

In addition to taking advantage of the foregoing property tax strategies, owners can reduce their federal income tax by donating a conservation easement to a qualified land trust. By doing so, owners may promote long-term conservation goals while enjoying reductions in not only federal income tax but also estate tax burdens. Donating a conservation easement qualifies as a charitable deduction on federal income tax returns. The amount of the deduction depends on the property value reduction resulting from restrictions on land use imposed by the easement.

As a legal agreement negotiated by a landowner with a land trust or government agency, the conservation easement limits land uses to conserve the natural state of the land. Landowners in decades past found that conservation easements were an effective tool for protecting productive agricultural land in the path of widespread development near urban areas. Rising land values spurred by eager developers near cities on the eastern seaboard made it difficult for landowners to maintain their agricultural operations. Rising property tax burdens and estate tax liabilities increased financial strains for those resisting the temptation to convert their land to a higher valued use. In addition, those owners saw property-related costs rising rapidly because of urbanization. With a conservation easement, however, farmers and ranchers could reap part of the financial benefits offered by conversion to urban uses. The benefit of voluntarily donating an easement came in the form of a charitable deduction from federal income taxes. The land remained agricultural, the value reduction limited potential property tax liabilities, and future generations had considerably lower estate tax liabilities.

The current income tax benefit depends on the value of the rights transferred by the easement. For example, a rancher forgoing development could continue some ranching activities but would surrender the right to develop residential or commercial sites on the land. By giving up the rights to develop, the landowner has essentially contributed those rights to the land trust. An appraiser could estimate the value of those rights by first conducting a property appraisal based on current market values before creating the easement. Presumably, that value reflects a contribution derived from development potential. The appraiser would then estimate the land value without development rights. The difference between those amounts represents the value of the easement and thus the amount of the charitable deduction gained by its donation.

For example, suppose a ranch was valued at three million dollars before the granting of an easement and only one million dollars thereafter. A two-million-dollar charitable deduction would thus be available. Obviously, the owner would need a substantial taxable income to realize the value of that deduction. At one time, IRS provisions limited annual deductions to 30 percent of adjusted gross income in any single year. Owners could roll over any remaining deduction amount in succeeding years, subject to the 30 percent limitation. Owners had to use up the entire deduction in the next five years, creating a six-year deduction opportunity window. Any amount of deduction remaining unused after the sixth year would expire. Obviously, owners with modest taxable incomes would likely realize only a fraction of sizable deductions under these regulations.

However, the Pension Protection Act of 2006 expanded the potential tax savings to landowners with modest incomes. Under the provisions of the act, allowable annual deductions increased to 50 percent of adjusted gross income each year. In addition, the window for deducting the balance expanded to fifteen years. Qualifying farmers and ranchers fared even better because the provisions allowed a deduction of up to 100 percent of adjusted gross income in any single year. A sizable deduction could wipe out their entire federal income tax liability for several years.

Unfortunately, these benefits applied only to donations made from

January 1, 2006, through December 31, 2007. Provisions of the farm bill passed in May 2008 extended those terms from January 1, 2008, through December 31, 2009. Congress extended those provisions through 2011. However, conservation groups continue to work to make the generous deductions permanent.

Many landowners view the conservation easement as a ruse designed to impose land use controls on future owners. This belief stems first from the fact that easements must apply in perpetuity to obtain the tax deduction and then from an abundance of stories about owners coming to rue their decision to donate an easement when disputes arose with the land trust over terms in the easement. Those stories, combined with a lingering distrust of many organizations operating land trusts and the limited tax deductibility, led many landowners to avoid conservation easements. Nevertheless, landowners desiring to preserve their land in its natural state should investigate the legal and financial implications of conservation easements. Even skeptics may find it tempting to consider donating an easement if Congress restores the more generous tax benefits.

Because the easement is permanent, any owner should investigate easement provisions thoroughly before proceeding. The owner must realize that the decision to permanently restrict the use of the property will preclude their children and grandchildren from selling the property to a buyer envisioning a higher valued use. From a purely investment perspective, the invested proceeds of the tax benefits should, over time, equal or exceed appreciation expected when developers' demand for the land emerges. That is the opportunity forgone when an owner permanently restricts land use. Many owners hesitate to foreclose future generations' options when they consider that their heirs may encounter the need to raise funds in an emergency. After analyzing this opportunity cost, some owners may opt to continue with the plan to donate an easement while others do not.

Negotiating an easement should begin with carefully choosing a team of professionals to structure the complex transaction so as to avoid potential difficulties should the IRS question the tax deduction. A carefully negotiated easement instrument will also help prevent unpleasant confrontations with the land trust by anticipating possible sources of contention.

Lawyers experienced with conservation easements can advise on negotiating the agreement and can draft the legal documents. Accountants can explain the tax implications of the charitable deduction. An appraiser can estimate the value of the easement to document the amount of the deduction. Choosing a competent professional team requires caution, however, because the IRS has become increasingly scrupulous in investigating. For example, it has questioned the accuracy of some appraisals used to justify sizable deductions for donated conservation easements.

For an owner to achieve a large tax deduction for a conservation easement, the negotiated agreement must restrict potentially valuable uses of the land. For example, a scenic ranch near a metropolitan area must exhibit a substantial value enhancement resulting from the potential for urban development. Forgoing that use represents a sizable financial sacrifice for the owner. For this kind of land, an owner could anticipate a substantial charitable deduction by donating a conservation easement. But a ranch with similar characteristics several hundred miles removed from any urban area would not have the same development potential, so a donated easement there would not result in a large tax deduction if an easement were granted. Giving up development rights in that instance might have little impact on land value, and owners of that kind of property should anticipate a much more modest charitable deduction.

Any appraiser documenting the deduction should carefully estimate the impact of development restrictions within the local market to justify their conclusions to the IRS. In Colorado, some landowners faced potentially sizable liabilities from disallowed deductions after the IRS questioned the accuracy of appraisals documenting the value of the donations. Some of the potential tax liabilities plus penalties may even exceed the value of these owners' lands should the IRS disallow the appraisals. To protect themselves, owners should use only attorneys, accountants, and appraisers with reputable professional credentials and substantial, successful experience with conservation easements.

Finally, given that granting a conservation easement in perpetuity is an irreversible step, owners should consider all of the implications for current and future generations. For more information on conservation easements, see

- "Land Locked," http://www.recenter.tamu.edu/pdf/1545.pdf
- "Conservation Easements Revisited," http://www.recenter.tamu .edu/pdf/1888.pdf
- Land Trust Alliance, http://www.landtrustalliance.org/
- Texas Land Trust Council, http://www.texaslandtrustcouncil.org/

For lists of land trusts, visit the following organization websites:

- Land Trust Alliance, http://www.findalandtrust.org
- Texas Land Trust Council http://www.texaslandtrustcouncil.org/
  index.php?option=com_content&view=article&id=101&Itemid=146

Environmental Incentives

The federal Conservation Reserve Program (CRP) and Environmental Quality Incentives Program (EQIP), as well as various state-sponsored initiatives, offer landowners opportunities to take advantage of revenue-enhancing or cost-reducing grants. Most environmental incentive programs either directly pay owners to undertake desirable management activities or share the cost of developing targeted improvements to the land. The programs generally strive to advance a particular policy-driven goal, such as retiring highly erodible land from farming and converting it to grassland. That effort, under the CRP, presumably leads to a reduction in erosion to the benefit of all.

CONSERVATION RESERVE PROGRAM

The Farm Service Agency (FSA) administers the Conservation Reserve Program (CRP), which is designed to remove fragile cropland from production and promote the growth of a permanent vegetative cover such as grasses or trees. Landowners volunteer to participate and face a competitive application process. In return, a landowner accepted into the CRP receives annual rental payments, as well as up to 50 percent of the cost of undertaking approved conservation practices, like planting permanent grasses or trees on the subject land.

Eligible land must be cropland that was farmed in four of the preceding six years or that comprised marginal pasturelands. In addition, the owner must have owned or operated the land for at least twelve months prior to the end of the sign-up period. Exceptions to this ownership requirement apply in the case of inheritance or foreclosure.

Owners may apply for the program during designated periods for general enrollment. The FSA does not open the program for enrollment every year; for example, it accepted enrollments in 2006 and again in 2010. Going forward, the program seeks to maintain a total of thirty-two million acres, and the FSA will likely schedule further enrollment periods when a volume of existing contracts expire and the associated acreage exits the program.

Owners must submit CRP applications at local FSA offices to be considered for enrollment in the program. In the application, owners submit a bid for a specified lease amount and an estimate of costs to convert the land to permanent vegetative cover. Before the sign-up, the FSA calculates a maximum rent for CRP acreage based on soil productivity and rents for dryland in the area. The FSA then compares the potential environmental benefits on a particular owner's land with land from competing owners to select those lands to be admitted to the program. The FSA ranks each application using a calculated environmental benefits index (EBI). The FSA makes offers based on the EBI ranking and the acceptability of the rental rate offered in the application. Factors considered in developing the EBI include:

- Wildlife habitat benefits
- Water quality benefits
- On-farm benefits
- Benefits enduring beyond the contract period
- Air quality benefits
- Costs

Owners often specify a rental payment below the maximum to increase their chances of being chosen to participate in the program. Once accepted to the program, the landowner must comply with the terms of the contract, undertaking required practices to ensure a viable vegetative cover on the erodible land. Contracts generally run for ten or fifteen years.

ENVIRONMENTAL QUALITY INCENTIVES PROGRAM

Another source of landowner income support is through a federal program that strives to "promote agricultural production and environmental quality as compatible goals." The Environmental Quality Incentives Program (EQIP) provides payments to landowners when they adopt approved environmental practices on their land. The EQIP initiative is the largest program designated for working agricultural lands. Landowners not participating in another government incentive program such as the CRP may find it beneficial to apply for the EQIP.

The EQIP involves a number of subprograms, including the Organic Initiative, Conservation Innovation Grants (CIG), and the Agricultural Water Enhancement Program (AWEP), each focused on specific conservation objectives. The EQIP operates through cost-share agreements with agricultural producers. The contracts outline planned implementation of conservation practices designed to address environmental natural resource challenges. The program encourages producers to use innovative technologies and cost-efficient methods to provide environmental benefits.

The EQIP provides both financial and technical assistance to farmers and ranchers who encounter threats to the soil, water, air, or other natural resources on their land. In 2010, Texas EQIP administrators announced that resource concerns included

- Animal waste management
- Sheet and rill water erosion control
- Grazing land productivity
- Irrigation water use
- Air quality
- Fertilizer use
- Wildlife habitat
- Energy
- Conservation tillage
- Carbon sequestration

For more information on the EQIP in Texas, see http://www.tx.nrcs .usda.gov/programs/eqip/eqipworks.html

Each of the resource concerns listed above has an associated set of activities that could qualify for EQIP cost sharing. For example, for animal feeding operations in Kerr County the NRCS air and water quality concerns resulted in the following list of "Eligible Practices" that landowners qualifying might implement and thus be able to gain financial assistance from EQIP:

- Atmospheric resource quality management
- Closure of waste impoundment
- Diversion
- Fence
- Field border
- Filter strip
- Grassed waterway
- Heavy use area protection
- Irrigation pit or regulating reservoir (storage tanks)

- Irrigation system, sprinkler
- Irrigation water conveyance (pipeline)
- Irrigation water management (for chemigation valves and flow meters)
- Manure transfer
- Nutrient management
- Pasture and hayland planting
- Pond sealing
- Pumping plant
- Sediment basins
- Terrace
- Waste storage facility
- Waste treatment lagoon
- Waste utilization
- Windbreak/shelter belt establishment

For more information on 2010 local EQIP concerns, see http://www
.tx.nrcs.usda.gov/programs/EQIP/10/index.html.

The EQIP has two separate pools of funding. The primary pool is general EQIP aid. General payments are limited to $300,000 per person or entity for all contracts entered into during any six-year period. The secretary of agriculture may raise the limitation to $450,000 for projects of special environmental significance, such as those involving methane digesters, which break down animal by-products into useful resources such as energy. Once accepted into the program, the producer receives a payment representing 75 percent of the cost of practices undertaken. The secondary pool promotes organic production. Payments to organic producers can amount to a maximum of $20,000 per year or $80,000 during any six-year period. Additionally, under both types of aid, EQIP offers priority payments for socially disadvantaged and limited resource producers; these payments may total up to 90 percent of the costs of installing or implementing a conservation practice. These participants can also receive advance payments of up to 30 percent of the anticipated costs incurred to purchase materials or to contract services to implement a practice.

Eligible applicants are not guaranteed a grant. An owner must compete with others for the limited funding. NRCS ranks applicants based on a number of factors, including the environmental benefits and cost-effectiveness of the proposed measures. EQIP assistance can vary from state to state or even from county to county.

Once accepted into the program, participants work with NRCS to develop an EQIP plan outlining specific conservation and environmental objectives, as well as a schedule for execution. The plan becomes the basis of the EQIP contract between the NRCS and the participant. The NRCS provides conservation practice payments to landowners based on the terms negotiated in the contract. EQIP contracts vary in duration from a minimum of one year after implementation of the last scheduled practice to a maximum of ten years.

The EQIP has benefited a number of Texas landowners. For additional information and details on the application process, landowners interested in participating should visit the program website, http://www.nrcs.usda.gov/PROGRAMS/EQIP/.

OTHER PROGRAMS

Numerous public and private programs offer assistance to owners undertaking targeted management practices on their land. Owners may find it beneficial to participate in these other programs. For information on several such programs, see http://www.texasagriculture.gov/GrantsServices/GrantsandServices.aspx and http://www.tpwd.state.tx.us/landwater/land/private/.

The New Risks of Ownership

10

A herd of Angus cattle descended from cows imported to the Hillingdon Ranch more than one hundred years ago on the hills near Comfort. Photograph by J. P. Beato III

The quest to own rural land in Texas follows a long and arduous trail. At the conclusion, the quest delivers land into the hands of the buyer whose envisioned use has the highest value. Having taken pains to methodically study all options, the new owner arrives at the end of the process with the assurance that the transaction represents the right risk taken to deliver the anticipated returns of landownership. The exercise systematically evaluated the impact of physical, legal, economic, and social influences on the buyers' envisioned ownership experience. Along the way, the buyer gained an understanding of the various sources of risk affecting landowners. This thorough examination of potential risks allowed the buyer to either limit exposure to various threats or prepare to address problems as they arise. At this stage, the buyer has secured at a reasonable price a property that is suited to his or her purposes. In addition, the transfer has delivered ownership of sufficient property rights to achieve the owner's goals.

Having successfully navigated the risk-laden transaction process, an owner's work to transform the land begins in earnest. As the new owner sets out to bring his or her vision to fruition, risk continues to threaten the project. Now the owner faces a different array of possible threats. For example, a kind-hearted owner planning to create a wildlife refuge might ban all hunting on a high-fenced property. The purpose of the plan was to allow the white-tailed deer population to prosper in a peaceful environment. After several years, the population will very likely expand to the point that it outstrips the ability of the land to provide enough nutrition to support the herd. The deer will literally destroy their habitat by eating everything in sight. What began as a vision of magnanimous kindness becomes a nightmare of denuded soil and starving animals. The management practices failed to achieve the vision of a peaceable kingdom because the owner misunderstood the role of the mechanism maintaining the balances needed to preserve wildlife populations in a healthy state. The overgrazing exposed soils to erosion and visited challenges to the health of the deer herd. Information provides the best protection against this new source of management risk. While well-managed land can provide substantial rewards for an owner, that owner must take proactive steps to become well informed about the consequences of specific management options to effectively transform the land into a more highly prized condition.

Appropriate actions can yield positive results that enhance property values. For example, one West Texas landowner had a ranch that provided an attractive landscape, but steep-walled canyons crisscrossed the ranch, limiting access to many parts of the property. So the owner invested substantial sums to construct good quality roads on the ranch. Before the road improvements, much of the land was accessible only by ATV, horseback, or by undertaking lengthy drives over public roads to enter the other side of the property. Establishing access within the confines of the ranch rewarded the owner with a more usable ranch and doubled the market value. Although the improvements required a substantial sum to complete, the new roads forever changed the character of the site. The owner risked a substantial sum but realized a sizable gain from the transformation.

Measures needed to establish owners' intended uses range from sustaining current conditions to reshaping the countryside to supporting desired activities like hunting, birding, or restoring native plants. Each change threatens to damage future conditions on the land if an owner undertakes them without sufficiently researching the likely outcome. Effectively supervising activities on a ranch or farm to avoid damaging the land while aspiring to reach a desired end requires judicious stewardship. Speaking of the family-owned Hillingdon Ranch, landowner/ranch manager Robin Giles observed, "The land doesn't really belong to us. We belong to it."

His remark reveals a deep respect for the biological and physical processes taking place on the land. Further, it reveals an appreciation of the responsibilities that come with ownership. The conscientious landowner should recall the envisioned use and exit strategy that guided their property search. The task now focuses on making those desired conditions a reality. To that end, the new owner will find that managing the land requires continuously learning about how to appropriately shape the natural processes taking place on the land. Farm and ranch owners must study a wide variety of information to appreciate and understand the intricacies of the ecological system and how the land's health depends on proper land management. Flawed management can inflict lasting damage that may require years of costly rehabilitation to repair.

If the envisioned use for the land requires reshaping the countryside, those changes imply the need to invest time and money. To evaluate the wisdom of adopting potential practices, the new owner should compare the costs against the effect on property value. When a contemplated practice does not enhance value beyond its cost, the market has suggested that most potential landowners consider the practice a mistake. That does not mean an owner should not adopt the practice, but it should cause a prudent owner to review the plan with a critical eye toward the need for such an activity. Perhaps the owner should consider forgoing that change. If the value enhancement falls short, an owner may opt to proceed anyway when he or she personally places great value on the outcome. However, a cost-benefit analysis helps an owner to avoid undertaking actions that may not contribute to a property's general appeal.

In general, improvements and activities designed to enhance the wildlife on a Texas ranch can boost property values. Management strategies often seek to establish and support a genetically improved wildlife population in an appropriate configuration of habitat. Adding high fences can contribute to that effort. On a property of sufficient size, adding high fences, establishing wildlife management plans, adding lakes, enhancing creeks, and adding ponds all can add value.

Enclosing a ranch with a high fence provides an example of a cost-benefit exercise. An owner can realize gains from installing a high fence as part of an established wildlife management plan, if the property is of sufficient size. In 2009 markets indicated that high fences intended to support established wildlife have varying impacts on land values according to location and depending on the cost of the fencing. In the Rio Grande plain of South Texas, land markets typically saw 2009 values increase by $100 per acre for an efficiently sized operation. Fencing costs ranged from $15,000 to $20,000 per mile or about $53 to $71 per acre for a square 2,000-acre ranch. Clearly, a fence would have contributed more value than its cost for a property with these characteristics. At $15,000 per mile on a square 550-acre ranch, fencing costs would have just about equaled the resulting value enhancement of $100 per acre. On a smaller acreage, the cost of a fence would surpass the value increase. If construction costs ran $20,000 per mile, the minimum size needed to justify the fencing cost would jump to 1,000 acres. Owners of smaller properties should know that the high fence would not pay for itself through value enhancement.

In the Hill Country, 2009 fencing costs were much higher, but additions to value were also higher. Because factors such as the cost of labor and materials and value enhancement vary depending on location, informed professionals in the area can help an owner by supplying current local information about what landowners can expect in terms of fencing costs and value increases.

An established wildlife plan that has produced results enhances land value, as do lakes stocked with bass. Installing these kinds of features can cost an owner a substantial sum. Analyses similar to the cost-benefit comparison for the high fence can help an owner choose among potential management activities and thus take the right risks.

There are many sources of information that will assist new landowners with management challenges. Neighboring landowners with established plans frequently can contribute valuable insights gleaned from their years on the land. New owners may find that they need ask only a few questions to find solutions to seemingly baffling problems.

Realizing that the health of wildlife populations in Texas critically depends on the actions of private landowners, the Texas Parks and Wildlife Department maintains an active outreach to private landowners (http://www.tpwd.state.tx.us/landwater/land/private/). Land buyers can find a wealth of information at their fingertips, as well as active support in the form of technical guidance. In addition, TPWD supports the creation of voluntary wildlife management associations throughout Texas. In these associations, owners in an area cooperate across fence lines to maximize the health of the wildlife. Joining one of these associations opens a door to a substantial body of local knowledge about practices that work and those that do not. Such organizations are particularly helpful as large ranches are parceled out among multiple owners. Cooperation among the new owners can contribute to sustaining the optimal combination of habitat and wildlife.

Buyers should also seek resources like the *Hill Country Landowner's Guide* (2009) to learn about the pitfalls that await unsuspecting owners. Whether the buyer acquired a tract of pine timber or a cotton field or a ranch teeming with wildlife, resources are available to help him or her institute effective programs to maximize the benefits of the landowning experience. New landowners can benefit from lessons others learned the hard way and find a wealth of potential assistance from helpful organizations:

- Texas A&M University College of Agriculture and Life Sciences, which, in addition to offering degree programs, provides access to research by experts on virtually all phases of agriculture and land in Texas (http://www.agrilifesciences.tamu.edu)
- Texas AgriLife Extension, which provides extensive assistance through a network of specialists and communicates research to the

public through an impressive volume of publications, available at https://agrilifebookstore.org/
• Caesar Kleberg Wildlife Research Institute at Texas A&M University–Kingsville, which focuses on South Texas in research on all phases of wildlife management. Institute publications and personnel have valuable insight into what works and what does not. Although the institute's work concentrates on South Texas, its information is also valid in other parts of the state (http://www.ckwri.tamuk.edu/).
• Texas Parks and Wildlife Department, which maintains a private lands outreach program offering many valuable resources to the landowner striving to provide habitat for wildlife. Owners can learn about particular management activities on their land, issues affecting their property taxes, landowner liabilities, the nearest wildlife management association, and countless other elements designed to make their land management more effective.
• Texas Christian University Ranch Management Program, which provides information on all phases of running a ranch (http://www.ranch.tcu.edu/portal/intro.asp)

Having purchased property, new owners now set out to collaborate with nature to achieve the goals established at the outset of the buying process. Far from concluding an activity, the acquisition process has delivered owners to this new beginning as they seek to understand and support the acreage to which they now belong. As new Texas land stewards, they will join others to guide activity on their land and sustain an environment reflecting Texans' values in the twenty-first century. Current landowners have thus assumed the obligation to manage their land responsibly and deliver it intact to future generations. If they rise to that challenge, they will indeed have taken all of the right risks and maximized the wealth accruing to responsible husbandry of natural resources. Perhaps they can anticipate realizing the annualized 7 percent return that rewarded frontier Texans for their efforts.

SELECTED BIBLIOGRAPHY

Appraisal Institute. *The Appraisal of Real Estate*. 13th ed. Chicago: Appraisal Institute, 2008.

Estes, Harper, and Douglas Prieto. "Contracts as Fences: Representing the Agricultural Producer in an Oil and Gas Environment." *Texas Bar Journal* (State Bar of Texas), May 2010.

Fambrough, Judon. "Dibs! Understanding the Right of First Refusal." Publication No. 1907. College Station: Real Estate Center at Texas A&M University, 2009.

———. "Easements in Texas." Special Report, Publication No. 422. College Station: Real Estate Center at Texas A&M University, 2001.

———. "Hints on Negotiating an Oil and Gas Lease." Special Report, Publication No. 229. College Station: Real Estate Center at Texas A&M University, 2002.

———. "Minerals, Surface Rights and Royalty Payments." Technical Report, Publication No. 840. College Station: Real Estate Center at Texas A&M University, 2009.

———. "Texas Surface Water: Ownership and Uses." Publication No. 1508. College Station: Real Estate Center at Texas A&M University, 2009.

———. "Wind Rights and Wrongs." Publication No. 1856. College Station: Real Estate Center at Texas A&M University, 2008.

Fehrenbach, T. R. *Lone Star: A History of Texas and the Texans*. New York: American Legacy Press, 1983.

George, Henry. *Progress and Poverty: An Inquiry into the Cause of Industrial Depressions and of Increase of Want with Increase of Wealth*. 1879. New York: Robert Schalkenbach Foundation, 2006.

Gilliland, Charles E. "Blazing the Preservation Trail: King Ranch's Legacy of Wildlife Stewardship." Publication No. 1855. College Station: Real Estate Center at Texas A&M University, 2008.

———. "CCNs: Legislation Tackles Inconveniences." Publication No. 1780. College Station: Real Estate Center at Texas A&M University, 2006.

———. "Digging Up Dirt on Septic Systems." Publication No. 1456. College Station: Real Estate Center at Texas A&M University, 2001.

———. "Hillingdon Ranch: Preserving a Legacy." Publication No. 1925. College Station: Real Estate Center at Texas A&M University, 2010.

———. "H_2O Pollution Solution." Publication No. 1442. College Station: Real Estate Center at Texas A&M University, 2001.

———. "Ranching for Rookies." Publication No. 1845. College Station: Real Estate Center at Texas A&M University, 2008.

Gilliland, Charles E., David Carciere, and Zachry Davis. "Texas Title Trail." Publication No. 1760. College Station: Real Estate Center at Texas A&M University, 2005.

Gilliland, Charles E., and Dan Daniels. "Seeing the Forest for the Trees . . . and Streams and Fish and Wildlife." Publication No. 1651. College Station: Real Estate Center at Texas A&M University, 2004.

Gilliland, Charles E., and A. Gunadekar. "Small, Medium, Large: Tract Size Affects Land Prices." Publication No. 1923. College Station: Real Estate Center at Texas A&M University, 2010.

Gilliland, Charles E., and D. Holland. "Big Gulp: Quenching Texans' Thirst for Water." Publication No. 1812. College Station: Real Estate Center at Texas A&M University, 2007.

Gilliland, Charles E., and M. Mays. "Endangered Species Act: A Landowner's Guide." Technical Report, Publication No. 1648. College Station: Real Estate Center at Texas A&M University, 2003.

Gilliland, Charles E., and N. Nichols. "Conservation Easements Revisited." Publication No. 1888. College Station: Real Estate Center at Texas A&M University, 2009.

———. "Downloading Dirt." Publication No. 1873. College Station: Real Estate Center at Texas A&M University, 2008.

Gilliland, Charles E., and James B. Vine. "Where the Deer and the Antelope Pay." Publication No. 1654. College Station: Real Estate Center at Texas A&M University, 2004.

Gilliland, Charles E., and Sarah Whitmore. "Cash for Conservation." Publication No. 1963. College Station: Real Estate Center at Texas A&M University, 2011.

Gilliland, Charles E., S. Whitmore, K. Wiehe, and A. Gunadekar. "Characteristics of Texas Land Markets—A Regional Analysis." Technical Report, Publication No. 1937. College Station: Real Estate Center at Texas A&M University, 2010.

Hoff, John K., and Jennifer L. Hoff. *Country Properties.* Houston: Seville Group, 1999.

Krome, Margaret, Teresa Maurer, and Katie Wied. *Building Sustainable Places: Federal Programs for Sustainable Agriculture, Forestry, Entrepreneurship, Conservation, and Community Development.* USDA, 2009. Free downloadable file.

Lea, Tom. *The King Ranch.* Boston: Little, Brown, 1957.

Ling, David C., and Wayne R. Archer. *Real Estate Principles: A Value Approach.* 3d ed. Boston: McGraw-Hill Irwin, 2010.

Mauro, Garry. *The Land Commissioners of Texas: 150 Years of the General Land Office.* Austin: Texas General Land Office, 1986.

Miller, Lloyd C. *Public Lands of Texas, 1519–1970.* Norman: University of Oklahoma Press, 1972.

Redmon, Larry A., and James C. Cathey. "Wildlife Management and Property Tax Valuation in Texas." SP-377, Texas AgriLife Extension Service, 2006. PDF file.

Rosenauer, Johnnie, Michael D. Hennessey, and James M. Mullen. *Farm and Ranch Marketing.* Upper Saddle River, N.J.: Prentice-Hall, 1998.

Stanley, Jim. *Hill Country Landowner's Guide.* College Station: Texas A&M University Press, 2009.

INDEX

Note: Page numbers in *italics* indicate photographs and illustrations.

96–97; fences, 113; on-site inspections, 69; Brazos River drainage, 31

bridges, 51

brokers, 47

Bryan, Texas, 15, 37

buildings on properties: appraisals, 49, 78; conservation easements, 23; locating suitable properties, 52–53; mapping services, 58–59, 60; property inspections, 67, 69; soil types, 53, 60

Caddo Lake, 52

Caesar Kleberg Wildlife Research Institute, 115

capital appreciation/gains, 8: price trends, 27, 29–30; risk analysis, 17; risk management, 10–11; tax-deferred exchanges, 23; tax-reduction strategies, 98

capital market risk, 12–13

Cathey, James, 100

cattle guards, 51

Central Texas, 38

certificates of convenience and necessity (CCNs), 90–91

charitable gifts/deductions, 22, 101–5

Clean Water Act, 13

closing deals, 96–109

clustering of properties, 30–31

College Station, Texas, 37

Colorado, 104

Comfort, Texas, 1

common ownership of land, 9

communities in proximity to land, 45

competing uses for land, 8. *See also* opportunity cost of land ownership

competition for properties, 34, 38–42

Concepción, Texas, 7

conservation easements, 21–23, 101–5

Conservation Innovation Grants (CIG), 106

Conservation Reserve Program (CRP), 105–6

consultants, 21

contracts, 96

conversion costs, 20

corporations, 22, 44

cost-benefit analyses, 113

costs of land ownership, 19–20, 97

county clerks, 78

credit, 12–13

croplands: conversion costs, 20; the environmental incentives, 105–6; investment value of lands, 20; proportion of statewide rural lands, 32; risks of land ownership, 9, 10–11, 12; searching for properties, 3, 31. *See also* dryland croplands; irrigation and irrigated lands

crops, 3

Czech immigrants, 7

Dallas, Texas, 7

Department of the Interior, 81

development of land: conservation easements, 21–23, 101–5; division of land among heirs, 22; exit strategies, 19; size of land parcels, 39–41; water resources, 90–91

division of land among heirs, 21

Doane's Agricultural Services, 74

downside risk, 10

drainage, 68, 81

dryland croplands: Austin-Waco-Hill Country region, 38; Far West Texas region, 35; Gulf Coast-Brazos Bottom region, 36; Northeast Texas region, 36; Panhandle-South Plains region, 34, 34; proportion of rural lands, 32; proportion of statewide rural lands, 31; South Texas region, 37, 37; West Texas region, 35, 35 easements: closing deals, 97; conservation easements, 21–23, 101–5; mineral leases, 80–81; for oil and gas operations, 92–94; risk-assessment, 45

East Texas, 43, 58. See also Northeast Texas region

economic conditions: capital market risk, 12–13; checklist for, 74–75; financial crises, 27–28; financial markets, 12–13, 14; Internet resources on, 74; local, 72; national, 72, 73; opportunity cost of land ownership, 19, 44, 103; price trends, 25, 25–29, 27, 29–30, 71; risk assessment, 45; size of land parcels, 42; of Southwest region, 73; of Texas, 73–74

educational programs, 46–47

Edwards Aquifer Authority (EAA), 13–14, 87

electrical lines, 81

El Paso, Texas, 35

Emory Peak, 61, 62, 63, 64

emotional involvement in land ownership, 19–20

Endangered and Threatened Animals of Texas (Campbell), 82

endangered species, 81–82, 83, 87

Endangered Species Act (ESA), 81–82, 83, 87

Environmental Protection Agency (EPA), 13

environmental protection and hazards: assessment of properties, 52; conservation easements, 101–5; environmental incentives, 105–6, 106–9; motivations for land purchases, 2; on-site inspections, 66; prior contamination, 81; risks associated with environmental regulations, 13; tax-reduction strategies, 99–100; wildlife management practices, 111. See also wildlife management lands

Environmental Quality Incentives Program (EQIP), 106–9

Espada, Texas, 7

ethnic composition of Texas, 7

evaluation of properties: mapping service, 56–65; on-site inspections, 65–67. See also appraisal of land

exit strategies, 18–23, 27, 42

family-owned lands, 17, 20–23

Farm and Ranch Contract Form, 96

Farm Credit Bank (FCB), 13

farming: historical uses of land, 6–8; motivations for land purchases, 2; regulatory risks, 13; risk analysis, 16; tax-reduction strategies, 98–99. See also agricultural lands; dryland croplands; irrigation and irrigated lands

Farm Service Agency (FSA), 57, 105–6

Far West Texas region: counties comprising, 33; proportion of land types in, 35, 35; proportion of statewide rural lands, 32; size of land parcels, 40; volume of sale in, 34

federal income tax, 97, 101–5

Federal Reserve, 72, 73

fencing land, 113

financial crises, 27–28

financial markets, 12–13, 14

finding properties: identifying suitable properties, 50–54; process overview, 44–45; searching resources, 45–50

fishing, 114

foreclosures, 26

foreign demand for land, 26

"for sale" signs, 50

Fort Hood, Texas, 38

Fredericksburg, Texas: orchard lands, 31; settlers of, 7

French immigrants, 7
fuel prices, 12
future market conditions, 16–18

Galveston, Texas, 37
game management, 12. *See also* wildlife
    management lands
gasoline prices, 12
gates, 51
General Land Office, 78, 79
George, Henry, 9
German immigrants, 7
Giles, Robin, 112
Graaskamp, James, 9–10
grazing lands: Panhandle-South Plains
    region, 34; proportion of rural lands,
    32; restricted-use lands, 44; risks of
    land ownership, 111; searching for
    property, 30–31; tax-reduction strate-
    gies, 97–98. *See also* improved pastures;
    native pastures
ground water, 87–92
groundwater conservation districts
    (GCDs), 13–14, 87–89, 92
Gulf Coast-Brazos Bottom region: coun-
    ties comprising, 33; proportion of
    land types in, 36, 36–37; proportion of
    statewide rural lands, 32; size of land
    parcels, 40; volume of sale in, 34, 34

habitat, 111. *See also* endangered species;
    wildlife management lands
Harrison County Courthouse, 76
heirs to property, 20–23
Hill Country: motivations for land pur-
    chases, 1; orchard lands, 31; propor-
    tion of land types in, 38; size of land
    parcels, 39; tax-reduction strategies,
    97–98
Hill County Landowner's Guide (Stanley), 114
Hillingdon Ranch, 110, 112
historical uses of land, 6–8, 54

homestead exemptions, 98, 100–101
Houston, Texas, 7, 37
hunting, 2, 17, 97–98

improved pastures: Austin-Waco-Hill
    Country region, 38, 38; Far West Texas
    region, 35; Gulf Coast-Brazos Bottom
    region, 36; Northeast Texas region, 36;
    Panhandle-South Plains region, 34;
    proportion of rural lands, 32; propor-
    tion of statewide rural lands, 31; South
    Texas region, 37; West Texas region, 35
improvements to properties: Kleberg on,
    6; market risk, 12; on-site inspections,
    65–66, 68; risk analysis, 17; value-
    enhancement, 53, 112
income from land: risk analysis, 11; risk
    management, 10; settlers, 7–8
inflation: competition for land, 8
information sources, 45–50
infrastructure: assessment of properties,
    51; on-site inspections, 68
inspections, on-site, 65–67
intended use of lands: endangered
    species, 82; mineral leases, 93; on-site
    inspections, 69; value-enhancing prac-
    tices, 112–15
interest rates, 12–13
Internal Revenue Service (IRS), 103
Internet searches, 49–50
investment value of land: conservation
    easements, 103–5; exit strategies,
    18–23; returns, 3. *See also* capital appre-
    ciation/gains
irrigation and irrigated lands: assess-
    ment of properties, 54; Austin-Waco-
    Hill Country region, 38; Far West Texas
    region, 35; Gulf Coast-Brazos Bottom
    region, 36; Northeast Texas region,
    36; Panhandle-South Plains region,
    34; proportion of rural lands, 32; pro-
    portion of statewide rural lands, 31;

cal uses of land, 6, 8; searching for property, 30–31; tax-reduction strategies, 97–98. *See also* improved pastures; native pastures

real estate brokers, 46–47

Real Estate Center (Texas A&M), 8, 73–74

real price of land, 25, 25–28, 29–30

Realtors Land Institute (RLI), 46–47, 49

recreational use of land: competition for land, 8; historical uses, 6–8; hunting, 2, 17, 97–98; mineral leases, 93; motivations for land purchases, 3; risk analysis, 11, 17; risk management, 10. *See also* wildlife management lands

Redmon, Larry, 100

regional depressions, 26

regional economics, 73

regional land markets, 32, 32–38, 33, 45–50

Regional Water Planning Groups, 91

rents, 19

Republic of Texas, 77

responsibilities of land ownership, 112–15. *See also* taxes and tax policy

restoration efforts, 2. *See also* environmental protection and hazards; preservation of lands

restrictions on use of lands, 36–38, 58. *See also* easements; leases

revenues from lands, 19, 97–98

right of first refusal, 80

rights of landowners, 80–81

Rio Grande region, 35, 113

risk associated with land ownership: assessing and managing, 111–15; capital markets, 12–13; cost-benefit analyses, 113; downside risk, 10; economic conditions, 44–45; exit strategies, 18–23; identifying suitable properties, 50–54; land speculation, 9–10; liquidity risk, 14; managing, 10–12; political/regulatory risk, 13–14; price fluctuations,

25–29; risk analysis, 11, 16–18; size of land parcels, 41; water rights, 90

roads, 51. *See also* access to lands

Round Rock, Texas, 38

royalty payments, 26

"rule of capture," 87

San Antonio, Texas, 87

San Antonio de Valero (the Alamo), 7

San José, Texas, 7

San Juan, Texas, 7

searching for properties: identifying suitable properties, 50–54; regions of the state, 30–31; useful resources, 45–50

septic systems, 66

settlers, 6–7

size-adjusted prices, 28

size of land parcels: price per acre, 29–30, 38–42, 40–41; water rights, 88–89

social growth, 9, 26

soils: assessment of properties, 52–53, 54; on-site inspections, 67; risk analysis, 11; Web Soil Survey (WSS), 57–60

Somerville, Texas, 5

South Texas region: counties comprising, 33; fencing costs, 113; proportion of land types in, 37; proportion of statewide rural lands, 32; size of land parcels, 40–41; volume of sale in, 34

Spanish rule of Texas, 77–78

Spanish settlers, 7

speculation in land, 9–10, 18

State of Texas, 77–78

stewardship ethic, 112–15

stock tanks, 86

structures on properties. *See* buildings on properties

suitable properties, identifying, 50–54

surface water, 85–87

surveys: closing deals, 96–97; land grants, 78; on-site inspections, 69; verifying ownership, 79 taxes and tax policy: conservation easements, 101–5; corporate tax structure, 44; environmental incentives, 105–9; 1031 exchanges, 22, 23; family-owned lands, 22; market impact of federal tax law, 26; regional land types, 31–32; risks of land ownership, 9; strategies to limit, 98–105; tax-reductions strategies, 97–98, 98–101; Texas Property Tax Code, 98, 100

Temple, Texas, 38

Temple-Inland, 44

Texas AgriLife Extension Service, 56, 114–15

Texas Alliance of Groundwater Conservation Districts, 92

Texas Alliance of Land Brokers (TALB), 47, 49

Texas A&M University, 8, 52, 73–74, 114–15

Texas and Southwestern Cattle Raisers Association, 74

Texas Christian University Ranch Management Program, 115

Texas Commission on Environmental Quality (TCEQ), 66, 85–87, 90–91, 92

Texas Comptroller for Public Accounts, 100–101

Texas Natural Resource Conservation Commission., 13

Texas Parks and Wildlife Department (TPWD), 82, 100, 114, 115

Texas Property Code, 67

Texas Property Tax Code, 98, 100

Texas Railroad Commission, 89

Texas Real Estate Commission, 96

Texas State Data Center, 74

Texas Supreme Court, 87, 92

Texas Water Code, 88, 89

Texas Water Development Board (TWDB), 87, 88, 91

threatened species, 81–82. *See also* endangered species

timber lands: Austin-Waco-Hill Country region, 38, *38*; corporate tax law, 44; Gulf Coast-Brazos Bottom region, *36*, 36–37; Northeast Texas region, 36, *36*; on-site inspections, 67; proportion of rural lands, 32; proportion of state-wide rural lands, 31

timing of land acquisitions, 27

title companies, 48

titles to land, 77–79, 97

topography: assessment of properties, 51; US Geological Survey, 60–64, *61*, *62*, *63*

total maximum daily loads (TMDLs), 13

toxic waste, 52, 81

transaction process, 111

transfer costs, 20

Trans-Pecos area, 24

uranium, 94

urban areas, 39, 102

US Department of Agriculture (USDA), 57–60

US Environmental Protection Agency (EPA), 13

US Fish and Wildlife Service (FWS), 81–82

US Geological Survey (USGS), 60–64, *61*, *62*, *63*

utilities: assessment of properties, 51, 53, 54; easements, 81; on-site inspections, 65–66

"vacancy" of lands, 79

Victoria, Texas, 37

volume of land sales, 25–29, *26*

Waco, Texas, 38

Washington County, 95

wastewater services, 90

water resources: assessment of properties, 45, 53–54; checklist for, 91–92;
developers, 90–91; environmental
incentives, 105–6; Environmental
Quality Incentives Program (EQIP),
106–9; ground water, 87–92; on-site
inspections, 68; regulatory risks,
13–14; risk analysis, 11; surface water,
85–87; water masters, 86–87; wells
and well water, 14, 87–89

Web Soil Survey (WSS), 57–60

wells and well water, 14, 87–89. *See also*
ground water

West Texas region: counties comprising,
33; proportion of land types in, *32, 35,
35;* proportion of statewide rural lands,
32; size of land parcels, *40;* value-
enhancing practices, 111–12; volume
of sale in, *34*

wetlands, 58

Wild Horse Desert, 37

"Wildlife Management and Property
Tax Valuation in Texas" (Redmon and
Cathey), 100

wildlife management lands: Austin-
Waco-Hill Country region, 38, *38;*
competition for land, 8; diversion of
surface water, 86; endangered species,
81–82, *81–83;* the environmental incentives, 105–6; Far West Texas region,
35; Gulf Coast-Brazos Bottom region,
36; market risk, 12; Northeast Texas
region, *36;* Panhandle-South Plains region, *34;* proportion of statewide rural
lands, *31;* risks of land ownership,
111; South Texas region, 37, *37;* tax-
reduction strategies, 100; Texas Parks
and Wildlife programs, 114; value-
enhancing practices, 113; West Texas
region, *35*

wind rights, 94

worst-case scenarios, 16–17